BIO-STRUCTURAL
ANALOGUES IN ARCHITECTURE

Joseph Lim

HAVERING
COLLEGE

BISPUBLISHERS

BIS Publishers
Building Het Sieraad
Postjesweg 1
1057 DT Amsterdam
The Netherlands

T +31 (0)20 515 02 30
F +31 (0)20 515 02 39
bis@bispublishers.nl
www.bispublishers.nl

ISBN 978-90-6369-204-9

Printed in China

To   Adam, Ryan, Graham & Ismurnee

Acknowledgements

I am grateful to the Department of Architecture, National University of Singapore in facilitating the research driven teaching and to Professor Heng Chye Kiang, Dean of the School of Design and Environment (SDE); Associate Professor Wong Yunn Chii, Head of the Architecture Department; and Professor Cheong Hin Fatt, former Dean SDE.

My sincere gratitude to Professor William Carmichael, Associate Professor K Tharmaratnam, Mr John Portwood, Professor Gulsum Nalbantoglu and to my colleagues for their encouragement and support.

Most importantly, to my students who believed in themselves when attempting the unfamiliar in learning.

TECHNOLOGICAL THINKING

Technology which is essentially instrumental in nature is dissociated from the original meaning implied in the Greek word *techne*. In Martin Heidegger's book, "Question Concerning Technology", *techne* is related to the notion of *poiesis*; its essence is not technological.[1] Marco Frascari argued that in the ontological dimension, an architect's drawings should demonstrate the technological image.[2] He defined a technological image as a reproduction in the mind of a sensation produced by a perception emerging from a critical system in which instrumental and symbolic representations are inseparable. This is evident in the detailing process which comprises both a constructive process that is primarily manual and operative (based on the logos of *techne*) and a rhetorical process which is mental and reflective in nature (based on the *techne* of logos). These dual processes characterise architecture as a discipline with a system of knowledge transferable into instrumental knowledge essential to the practice of construction.

However, in the 18th century Enlightenment period of science and reason, the rhetorical mode of thinking was replaced by the scientific. In architecture and engineering, the first Industrial Revolution brought on new construction techniques and structural material which generated an aesthetic, independent from timber and masonry precedent. Ways of 'seeing and constructing' were re-evaluated with the advent of industrialisation and new technology. Architecture struggled to establish its disciplinary basis with the separation of *techne* from the technique of construction.

Karl Botticher who sought an architectural theory involving the use of structural iron in the conception of space, distinguished between *kern-form* (the core form) and *kunst-form* (the art form).[3] The art form was intended to "symbolise the concept of structure and space which in its purely structural state could not be perceived". Related to this concept was the Semperian concept of tectonic which dealt with the product of human artistry and not with its utilitarian aspect, i.e., with the poetic revelations of the human attempt to express a cosmic order in moulding the material. Where *techne* includes "tectonic" and "type", tectonic describes the condition when architectural elements such as a column, wall, beam and roof transcend their structural rationality and reveal meaning. Here, Gottfried Semper meant the art form and the core form in a "structural symbolic" sense and not in a "structural-technical" sense.[4] Semper's concern was in reassessing and changing architectural forms which were established by tradition to match the means available with industrial fabrication.

Whereas architects were concerned with formulating new theories to replace those outmoded by mechanised building techniques and the use of new building materials, the engineer's mental framework has also transformed in ways which according to Antoine Picon corresponded to changes in the representation of nature and society and to technology as a form of social production in the 18th Century.[5]

Picon argued that the perception of the physical world changed from the classical version which considered nature as being organised according to the laws of order and proportion to one which characterised change and movement. Consequently, engineers in this tradition changed the basis of conception of the built environment from one which is based on geometrical knowledge to one which is based on mathematics and the sciences in the adoption of new spatial and constructive patterns. Beauty is no longer traditionally defined in reference to an object but in reference to the dynamic processes of construction.

In contrast to engineers who distinguish science from engineering, the 18th Century engineers saw a close relationship between science and technology. To bridge the gap between science and engineering, the French developed a form of engineering science which dealt with processes ranging from the harnessing of forces in nature for man's convenience to the organisation of labour for production and building. Coupled with this development was a new design approach to the processes of production as an organised sequence of technical operations.[6] Both developments emphasise the value of process and organisation in the aesthetics of things designed.

In the engineering context, viability is valued as a form of beauty attained through "aesthetics of process" instead of the traditional "aesthetics of object". Related to this definition of process-oriented design (as being different from one which is object-oriented) are forms of technological thought used by engineers.

REPRESENTATIONAL THINKING

Where the purpose of an architect's drawing is to contain the necessary data and instructions for construction, its format translates plan to tectonic articulation by means of scalar representation. The drawing is essentially a means to control the geometry when communicating intention to different parties involved in the construction process. Intrinsic in the representational means is a predetermined shape of spaces and material form which are composed in a process, prior to its representation. When the representational means becomes the media in which the design process operates, then the constructional/material system is constrained by the representational means. Unwittingly, seeing is not part of constructing, and is left out of representational intention.

In contrast to this limitation, the representation of a bubble box by PTW architects is interpreted as a three-dimensional steel network by Tristram Carfrae for the Beijing National Olympic Swimming Centre. Here, Carfrae's representation of the engineer's geometry is both structural and spatial in characterising its bubble imagery in ETFE. The geometry of the structure involved a process of faceting polyhedral elements to generate an asymmetrical three-dimensional pattern representing bubble intersections. This pattern was used to locate the compressive struts in space with the desired control in their length and intersections, to resist buckling and out-of-plane forces. The structure with trabeculae-like pattern was confined to the periphery of the swimming arenas enabling a free-span space within, whilst functioning as a cavity scaffold for the ETFE climatic filter. Such design processes incorporate structure in the representation of architecture. In design approaches of this kind, *the structure becomes the architecture*.

ASSOCIATIVE THINKING

Central to the idea of a design strategy in developing the architectural concept, is a form of technological thinking which drew inspiration from other forms of knowledge. In addition to scientific and empirical thinking which drove the development of modern building culture in the 19th Century, Tom Peters identified a third – associative form of matrix thinking.[7] Although it was scientific thinking which enabled the understanding of building materials and structure, Peters argued that it did not help builders design. Instead, builders created structures and processes in building through what he called associative or matrix thinking.[8]

Associative or matrix thinking is a multi-faceted thought form which allows ideas to be connected from different fields of knowledge in the formulation of definitive design solutions or decisions. Peters cites 19th Century examples of this form of design thinking which involved spatial and analogical translations of ideas into architecture of that time.

Charles Fox demonstrated a complex three-dimensional ability in thinking which related structural geometry with construction in framing the architectural space of Joseph Paxton's Crystal Palace.[9] Whereas the overall form of a building would be conceived as key transverse sections or typical cross-sections, Fox conceived the structure as a gridded module identical in two axes. This facilitated construction in two directions of the building. Like the Gothic cross vault structural bay, this module embodied both structure and space in its construction.

With Karl Ludwig Althans' Cast-Iron Sayn Foundry in 1830 and Marc Brunel's tunnelling shield for the Neva Bridge, Peters distinguished yet another form of associative thinking which was analogic in nature, and which derived ideas from one field of experience or knowledge to create design solutions in another.[10]

The two examples differed as a process in design. Whereas Althans used foundry artefacts as building structure, Brunel translated animal behaviour into the mechanical action for a tunnelling shield. The former process is improvisational in building assembly whilst the latter process involves the derivation of a mechanical analogue. Both approaches were unfettered by precedent and inventive in spirit. The analogues in nature were used to define a mechanical principle or a structural principle.

In the case of Robert Le Ricolais' research work, material configurations maximising structural strength were strategic to enabling minimal weight for maximum span applications in architecture. In designing the automorphic, the design process involves the abstraction of an analogue from a natural form, and finds a rapport between the derived forms that yields a hybrid or some connective relationship.[11]

Half a century after Fox and Paxton, D'Arcy Thompson wrote his mathematical and physical treatise of biological growth, explaining form as a diagram of forces acting on it or which have acted on it.[12] In analysing the form of complex creatures, he theorised two strategies:

> parts or wholes even when not shaped directly by physical forces, take optimal forms of ideal geometry as solutions to problems of morphology; and

> even if complex prototypes were to be accepted as generic, their transformations to related forms may be expressed as simple deformations of entire systems.

The experiments of Felix Candela, P.L. Nervi and Eduardo Torroja were enabled by ferrocement construction with forms rationalised by rigid shell systems and ribbing patterns modulated by a stiffening strategy analogous with natural shell structures. Robert Le Ricolais experimented with isotropy and material direction to develop rigid surface panels with high load to weight ratios.[13]

Later explorations by Frei Otto were enabled by membrane fabrics, lattice, masted and tension systems in imaginative translations of pneumatic and surface tension forces found in natural examples.

CURRENT DEVELOPMENTS

The interest in current design research relates to the concept of emergence in the fields of evolutionary biology, artificial intelligence, complexity theory, cybernetics and general systems theory. Michael Weinstock defines emergence in the sciences as relating to the production of forms and behaviour by natural systems that have an irreducible complexity.[14] The term also refers to the mathematical approach in modelling the processes in computational environments.

In architecture, the research is based on principles and dynamics of organisation and interaction, and which involves the mathematical laws governing natural systems for application in artificially constructed systems, as design strategies. Form and behaviour emerge from the processes of complex natural systems. These processes produce, articulate and maintain the form of natural systems which undergo dynamic changes with the environment. This implies that the structures of natural systems possess capabilities of adaptability and controlled dynamics. Given these characteristics, it is possible to discover prototypes which

transcend those of Euclidean geometries;

dissolve the constructional and functional differentiations between structure and envelopes in building;

suggest alternative structural types and their impact on new architectural space; and

enable the relation of material elements with social and physical environments through a process of material operations involving culture, climate and energy.

In structures, strategies are sought from nature for shape-optimising morphologies and the arrangement of components in complex hierarchies to provide multiple load-paths, and accommodating changes in environments which are both external and internal to the material system. Building envelopes may be considered as systems integral with structure, using panels to regulate environment in a geometry that can adapt to physical and climatic changes in the environment. The structures to these building envelopes are developed as surface elements with kinetic capacities to change geometry when triggered by environmental forces. The change in geometry can also increase structural capacity by sharing and distributing loads.

It may be observed that the multiplicity of natural organisms can be attributed to the specialisation of cellular tissue in performing differentiated tasks. Depending on their location within a large system and response to environmental stimuli (internal and external environments), simple elements may assume different functions through morphological adaptation.

Today, Michael Hensel and Achim Menges identify this principle in nature as a decisive shift from building systems to the notion of *"... differentiated material systems with self-organisational capacities that can be utilized across numerous scales from the material (constituent) to the performance of elements within the larger functional economy of an overall system...Here the model in architecture is derived from the study of differentiation and energy which relates pattern and process, form and behaviour, design and construction in forming a symbiotic relation with the natural world...."*[15]

Against this background of studying material systems and organisational structures in changing the way we think of structure and space, are questions concerning architecture. The design studios in this book are attempts at studying systems outside building, in this case nature, as a means to derive structural prototypes for exploring alternative forms of architecture.

Notes

1. Heidegger identified *techne* as the Greek word for technology and considered it both "poetic and revealing". *Techne* characterised the ontological relationship between object type and its logos of making.
2. Marco Frascari, "A New Angel/Angle in Architectural Research: The Ideas of Demonstration", Journal of Architectural Education (Volume 44, Issue 1, 1990)
3. Wolfgang Herrmann, "Karl Botticher's The Principles of Hellenic and Germanic Ways of Building", In what style should we build? (Chicago Press, 1992)
4. Calatrava's bowstring trusses in his Wohlen Music Hall roof are structural tied arches and metaphorical expressions of a string instrument at the same time.
5. Robert Fox (ed), "Antoine Picon's Towards a History of Technological Thought", Technological Change (Harwood Academic, 1996)
6. Tom F Peters offered a technological definition of beauty as one which was related to an aesthetics of process (instead of an aesthetics of the object) arguing that it was the broader view of an object in its spatial, functional, organisational context that was significant in determining its design aesthetics
7. Tom F Peters, Building the Nineteenth Century (MIT Press, 1996)
8. This is precisely why epistemological learning in the physical sciences does very little design studio application.
9. Charles Fox and John Henderson were the railway contractors who provided the manufacturing and construction expertise for the Crystal Palace designed by Joseph Paxton in 1851.
10. In the Sayn Foundry, the structural framework actively supported the mechanical devices used in the iron working process. The columns supported swivelling derrick cranes which pivoted on ball-bearings made of canon balls. The bottom chords of the trusses which were built as oversized laminated steel wagon springs supported the gantry used to lift the molten iron from the furnace to the casting floor.
11. Peter McCleary, "Robert Le Ricolais' Search for the Indestructible Idea", Lotus International 99 (Milan, 2000)
12. D'Arcy Thomson, On Growth and Form (Cambridge University Press, 1961)
13. Peter McCleary, "Robert Le Ricolais' Search for the Indestructible Idea", Lotus International 99 (Milan, 2000)
14. Michael Weinstock, "Morphogenesis and the Mathematics of Emergence", Architectural Design (Volume 74, Issue 3, 2004)
15. Michael Hensel and Achim Menges, "Differentiation in Nature and Design", Morpho-Ecologies (Architectural Association, 2006)

EXPERIMENTAL DESIGN STUDIOS

We are given an area which is to be covered, a space which is to be enclosed. We know the movement conditions of the external forces. If we set ourselves the task of sustaining these forces, by transferring the reactions to the supports in a simple manner by using the space-enclosing surface itself to carry the load ...this is a general, but, finally, the only interesting problem.
Bernard Lafaille[1]

One of the most difficult pedagogical problems in architectural studio design is the integration of structural thinking with architecture. For the student, the concerns of basic form-making usually eclipse any sophisticated investigation into structure. As a result, students often revert to "standard" structural systems (for example, portal or space frames) by default. Yet, even when a studio focuses specifically on structural issues, a gap can exist between the invention of structurally interesting form (form-making) and the verification of that form using statics as a means of analysis. Sometimes, structural understanding does not develop beyond adopting the visual manifestation of a structural system. In order to address this pedagogic difficulty, experimental design studios focused on the study of natural form as a basis for generating architectural structures. These studios were taught by the author to second year architecture students in the National University of Singapore.

The inventiveness and economy in the engineering of nature's structures serve as design strategy in optimising minimal resources for maximum effect. This is evident when all organisms compete for available energy and limited resources in order to grow, procreate and enhance survival. Related to the harnessing of limited resources for the survival of the organism is the way it structures itself in order to grow, assimilate and process energy to adapt to its physical environment.

The technological outcome of borrowing ideas from nature is termed biomimetics.[2] It was an aesthetic as much as it was a practical pursuit in the 19th Century.[3] Such thinking forms the basis of biomimetic processes by which useful ideas are abstracted from the living world because the underlying basis of reducing wastage through the effective deployment of physical material is common to biologists, engineers and architects in understanding form. Related to the physical and mathematical logic of designing structures are implicit design values of economy and simplicity in acquiring stability, strength and safety. Where the epistemic learning of theoretical aspects in building structures did not enable architecture students to apply it readily to architectural design, the architectural design process focused on a set of questions concerning stability and strength which were essentially configurational in nature and which related to the creation of space.

The design experiments started with an interesting premise. Rather than beginning with architectural or structural precedents in building, students instead studied the natural forms of living species. This lead to two results: a sculptural interpretation related to structural metaphor, and a structural interpretation related to a theoretical understanding of surface structures. Moreover, dynamic attributes of the living nature studied influenced these interpretations: such as their growth form and the motor abilities of these animals and their organs.

The works of D'Arcy Thompson and Frei Otto were used as references for nature's strategies in achieving strength in rigid tissue forms.[4] Robert Le Ricolais' documentation of his experimental research workshop at the University of Pennsylvania elucidates how analogical thinking advances structural ingenuity in the design process.[5] Fred Angerer's investigation into surface structures demonstrates that conceptual analogy can be linked with technical strategy in the structural articulation of load bearing surface forms.[6] All four authors explore the concept of minimum material for maximum strength and the relationship of geometric patterns to highly effective forms that resist compression and bending forces. These texts pioneer the ways in which surface structures might define space using a space-enclosing surface as the load-bearing element. B. Kresling's and Julian Vincent's work on mechanisms in biological deployable structures formed a reference for mechanisms enabling great degrees of movement and avoiding obstruction between moving elements.[7] These authors explored material strengthening forms and patterns in effective kinetic configurations.

In the initial phase of the studios, students were asked to select one type of living species for study on an individual basis. They each identified a significant geometric pattern in the skeletal structure that might reveal the resistance of compressive forces. Some students also looked for a biological characteristic of the living species entailing mechanical action or movement. The students then created an abstract analogue in the form of a structural model that related space and form to load or movement, as derived from each of their living species. These structural models specifically explored abstract geometries relating architectural form to the characteristics of the living species in a provisional way. In abstracting an analogue from natural form, the studio projects searched for a connection between pattern and structural action in a manner which related to overall configuration or locomotion.

Subsequent developmental models were tested and improved for structural and mechanical action and for the ability of these properties to change and to suggest space. Using live loads, models were tested to its carrying capacity before buckling. Attributes of the model (for example, the direction of folds in relation to the direction of forces) could then be modified and re-tested for improved strength. These developmental models eventually led to "prototypes" or architectural elements that would have the potential – outside the immediate aims of the studio -- to be incorporated into a real site and a real program.

Innovation in form-making, and structural efficiency, were the main criteria for the evaluation of the prototypes. Lightweight prototypes that were best able to maximise rigidity and resist buckling under loading were considered to be the most successful. The students' intuitive and theoretical understanding of the structural form was also carefully assessed. Other criteria were considered as well. For instance, the degree to which structural action advantaged architectural space while maintaining a reference to mechanical principle of the originating living species morphology was important. Similarly, the extent to which this form geometrically increased the stability and strength of the prototypes was of equal significance. The sculptural quality of the prototype was also an aesthetic that was evaluated for its ability to define architectural space.

Notes
1. Bernard Lafaille, *Vorbericht zum zweiten Congress der Internationaler Vereinigung fur Bruckenbau und Hochbau* (October 1936)
2. Julian F.V. Vincent, "Stealing Ideas from Nature", Deployable Structures (ed. S. Pelligrino) (Springer, Vienna)
3. Philip Ball, "Life's Lesson in Design", Nature 409 (London, 2001)
4. D'Arcy Thomson, On Growth and Form (Cambridge University Press, 1961); Frei Otto, Frei Otto: Structures (London, Longman, 1972)
5. Peter McCleary, "Robert Le Ricolais' Search for the Indestructible Idea", Lotus International 99 (Milan, 2000): p.101-131
6. Fred Angerer, Surface Structures Building (London, Norman Press Ltd, 1961)
7. Julian F.V. Vincent, "Deployable Structures in Nature", Deployable Structures (ed. S. Pelligrino) (Springer, Vienna)

PLANT ANALOGUES

In this set of experiments, plant structures were studied as a basis for structural development using plant morphology as a reference for studying structural configuration in achieving strength through form. In particular, how movement, flexibility and resisting load related to cellular and tissue organisation.

Students selected monocotyledonous, dicotyledonous and aquatic plants for study. Their exploration fell into three categories: vertical structures, folding structures and floating structures.

In the first phase, students attempted to understand transpiration, photosynthesis and reproduction; and researched plant biology in respect of their classification, general, special types, structural strategies for food production and conveying water, accommodating movement, growth and reproduction. Students sought structural patterns in the overall configuration of the plant and in its element parts, which form an overall strategy in achieving strength through shape.

Biological studies covered an interesting scope of plant life: leaf growth was studied as a pattern strategy to minimize self shading in a tree to maximize photosynthesis. Leaf cell patterns were also studied as a transformable surface. Most significantly, the growth of rigid and soft tissue to enable both flexibility and rigidity in plant stems, branches and vines served as useful design strategies in configuring vertical structures. These studies were translated into initial models representing form and structure.

In the second phase, structural models were developed from initial models in the first phase, and were tested to study how they deformed under load. Another set of projects developed kinetic models and their effectiveness was measured in terms of their capacity to change the area of sheltered space. Configurational modifications were made to improve stiffness and strength.

Studies in other cases focused on joint and support design which amplified kinetic movement with a potential to accommodate a range of architectural programmes. These were necessary to contextualise further design development of the structural idea.

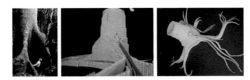

FAMILY *ARECACEAE*
Genus *Dyptis madagascariensis* (*Madagascar* Palm)

Buttress roots have a wide-spreading, tapering growth pattern, and are able to resist wind and lateral load through planar, triangulated cross-sections. This idea was explored in developing a structural module for a space with a height of 30m. In attaining height in the structure, the challenge was to shape support elements to resist buckling without incurring physical girth. Following the strategy of buttress roots in tall trees, the base of the column was widened and configured as a tripod whilst the mid-section was shaped in three "buttress elements" meeting in the central axis of the column. The stems of the *Madagascar* palm leaves cantilevered in an overlapping manner from the centre of the plan in a radial pattern. In the prototype, the transverse elements fanned outward at the upper portion of the "stem" to become a canopy, forming structural roof cantilevers. Load tests were carried out to identify weak parts of the structure. In increasing the load-bearing strength of the structure, five modifications were necessary throughout load testing. The strutting of the structural members were intended to create patterns sympathetic to the overall form and shape of the entire module. The individual structural modules were then combined in a series of patterns to study their effect on defining space with the clear spans achieved. Configurations 3 and 4 created the widest distances between vertical supports but secondary roof forms would be necessary to span the gaps between the module roofs.

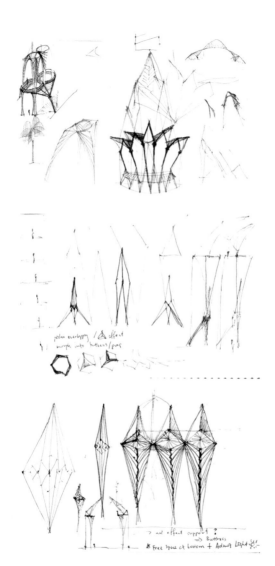

polar overlapping / offset
morph into buttress / piers

not offset support ?
→ Buttress
free space at bottom + admit light

23

Long buckling length at the mid portion. Little space is encompassed in relation to height of structure.

Y-strutting to increase stiffness Additional member to transfer loa down to base.

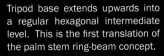

Tripod base extends upwards into a regular hexagonal intermediate level. This is the first translation of the palm stem ring-beam concept.

Further extension at 3 points spread the top portion. Lines forces are directed back down the tripod base.

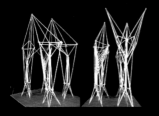

Attempts to spread the canopy.

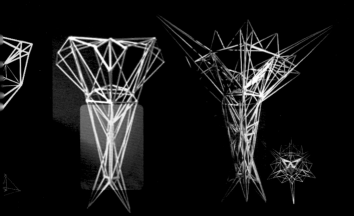

The 3-pt extension is tied together, forming the second translation of the ring-beam concept. The 3 points arch outwards from the elevation forming a canopy.

Final roof form with struttings at the mid portion configured after load test.

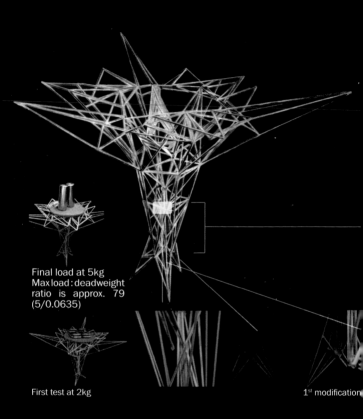

Final load at 5kg
Max load : deadweight
ratio is approx. 79
(5/0.0635)

First test at 2kg

1st modification

First test at 2kg
Members detached and buckled

1st modification
Model was stable at 2kg. At 4kg, model held for 30 sec before buckled
and snapped at base.

2nd modification
Model was stable at 4kg with signs of buckling observed.

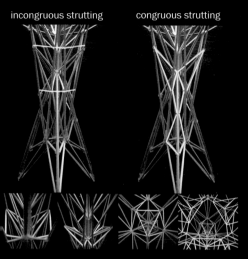

incongruous strutting   congruous strutting

Details of the designed congruous strutting pattern
and its intensification at different levels.

2ⁿᵈ modification   3ʳᵈ modification   4ᵗʰ & 5ᵗʰ modifications

3ʳᵈ modifcation - double beam inserted
Model was stable at 4kg. One strut gave way but it did not buckle.
Slight twisting at upper portion of model observed.

4ᵗʰ modification - thickened centre of double beam
Twisting observed at 4.5kg but base remained stable.

5ᵗʰ modification - strutting at mid portion
Slight twisting observed at 5kg.

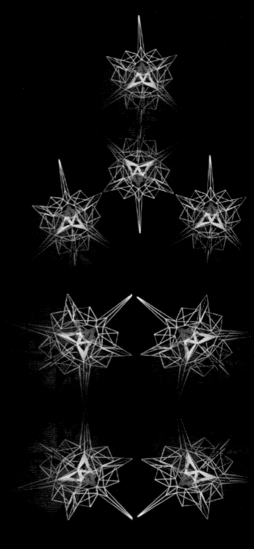

Configuration 1

Configuration 3

Configuration 2

Configuration 4

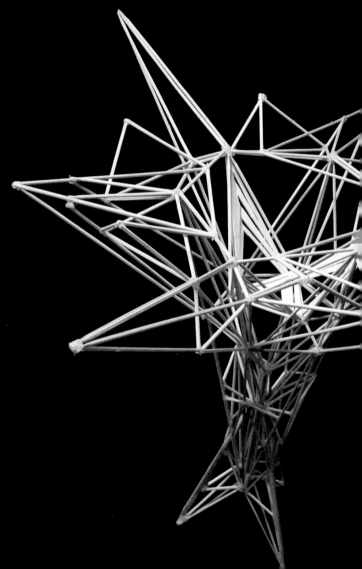

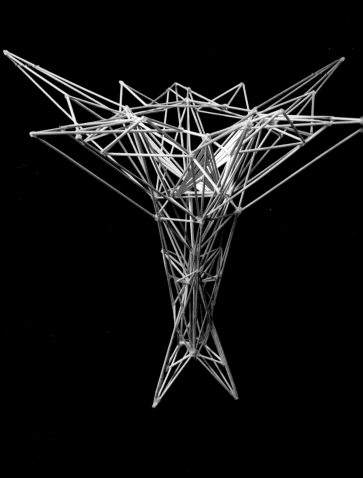

FAMILY *ARECACEAE*
Genus *Dyptis madagascariensis* (*Madagascar* Palm)

Despite the massive load of *Madagascar* palm's widespread leaves, the cantilever gains support from the leaf beneath by the manner the latter wraps the former leaf sheath with stiff, brownish, woolly fibres. Bamboo stick models were first used in attempt to simulate similar curved forms of palm leaf sheath, to form a prototype unit, employed in different configurations in the final structure. In subsequent load models, timber gridshells in the shape of hyperbolic paraboloids replaced the stick prototype unit as structural interpretations of the palm sheath. The two final configuration of gridshells were applied to linear and central plan forms. Structurally, the form is efficient in attaining strength through its shape, thus achieving a structure that spans over wide spaces with a small sectional thickness of material. It acts like a lattice shell, such that the saddle roof is subject to both compression and tension. Under load, the two layers of wooden strips at diagonals to each other were to function as opposing weaves, each transferring forces to the thicker perimeter compression member. Connections between the shells and wood ties were expressed in the form of mortise and tenon joints. This allowed the wood joint to be both tight and relatively inconspicuous. However, the two layers of thin wooden strips buckled when the structure was loaded and separated. This was because the wood strips used were too stiff to be woven together. Bamboo strips as an alternative, could be woven to effectively increase the surface strength of the structure.

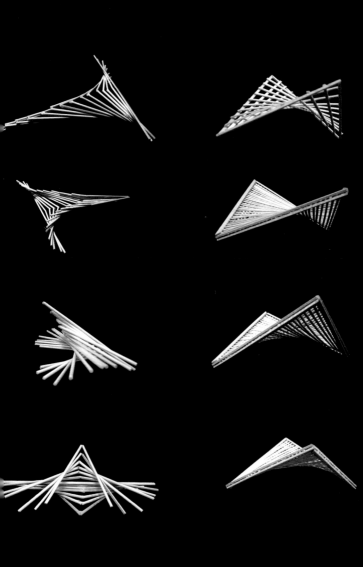

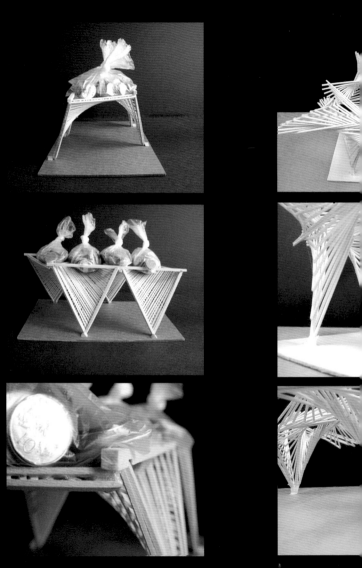

FAMILY *BETULACEAE*
Genus Carpinus betulus (Hornbeam leaf)

The hornbeam tree grows in temperate zones. There are different variations of the species found in Europe and North America. The leaf is folded in the bud scales during the winter and is folded like a series of parallelograms. This results in a system that allows the leaf to be "pushed out" from a single driving point. The folding pattern can be likened to a corrugated sheet, the folded profile enhances the rigidity of the lamina.

The initial models were modelled closely to the pattern of the leaf itself. Later models were based on variations of parallelograms. The first initial model had an angled corrugation that allowed it to open and fold up. This angled corrugation also enhanced the stiffness of the model. Another initial model had a different size panel, though still a parallelogram. As the model opened out, the corrugation got flatter and less pronounced. This meant the canopy would get less stiff and tend to bend over. The hornbeam leaf overcomes this by growing the central leaf vein straight.

The unfolding pattern was studied when individual "leaves" of varying proportions were joined side by side. This combined configuration was more efficient as the entire canopy could be made to unfold by applying a force at one point. When the shape of individual panels varied whilst maintaining their fold angles, openings were possible in the surface of the canopy as it folded. This could be used as skylights or "windows" in exterior surfaces.

The final configuration had two different size panels. All parallelograms had similar angles. The result was a configuration that allowed light and air through openings that could vary in size when the roof moves in a horizontal direction. The drawings showed the canopy in stages of unfolding in elevation and plan. In elevation, the canopy grew longer and also flatter as it unfolded. In plan, it covered a greater area as it unfolded. As it was necessary to move the canopy on tracks which were supported on beams, this study enabled the trajectory of the panel vertices as the canopy unfolded. Beams would be shaped according to the trajectory to enable rollers on tracks to move the canopy panels. The middle of the canopy is designated as the point at which force is applied to move the roof. This point moves only up and down and an actuator such as a hydraulic piston can be used to activate the canopy from this point.

Images of the canopy were taken in varying stages of unfolding and overlaid onto each other. This allowed the locus of the roof's lower vertices to be traced. The locus articulates the geometry of beam tracks on which roller wheels move. The canopy panels were connected via hinge pins where pins converged to another upright pin with a roller at the end. This roller would run along a C-channel track. The entire canopy rested on a series of bipod shaped columns to counter the lateral forces of the moving panels.

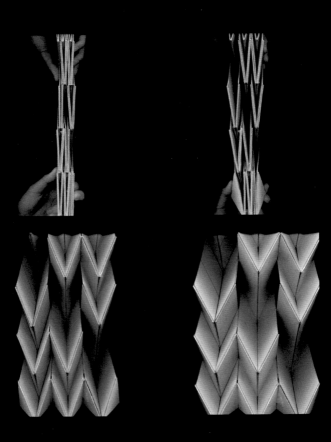

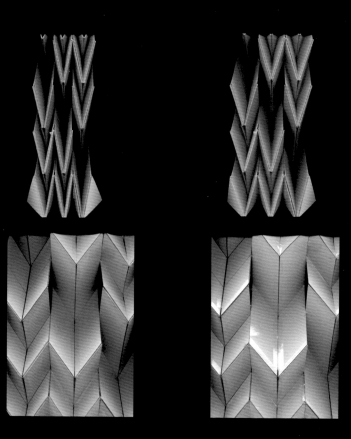

top view

bottom view with tracks in red

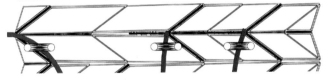

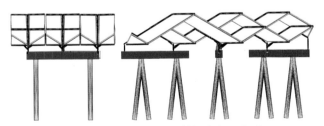

The entire canopy rests on a series of bipod-shaped columns
to counter the lateral forces of the moving panels

fixed point (the red dot)
the middle of the
canopy is designated
as the point at which
force is applied to move
the roof. This point
moves only up and
down and an actuator
such as a hydraulic
piston can be used to
activate the canopy
from this point.

loci (the red lines)
Images of the canopy
were taken in varying
stages of unfolding
and overlaid onto each
other. This allowed the
locus of the roof's lower
vertices to be traced.
The locus articulates
the geometry of beam
tracks on which roller
wheels move.

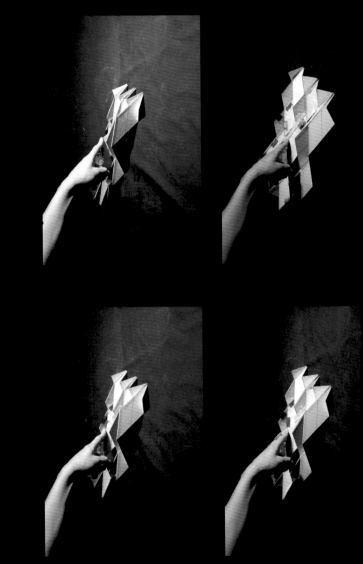

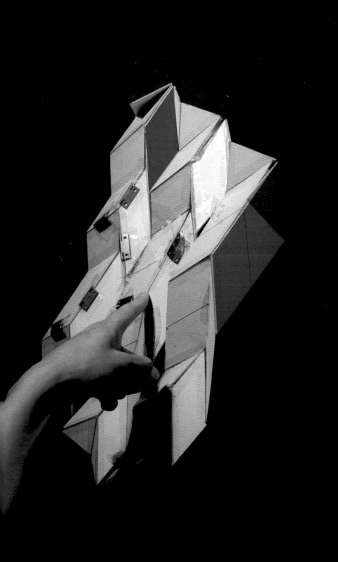

The final configuration has
two different size panels. All
parallelograms have similar
angles.

The result is a configuration
that allows light and air through
openings that can vary in
size when the roof moves in a
horizontal direction.

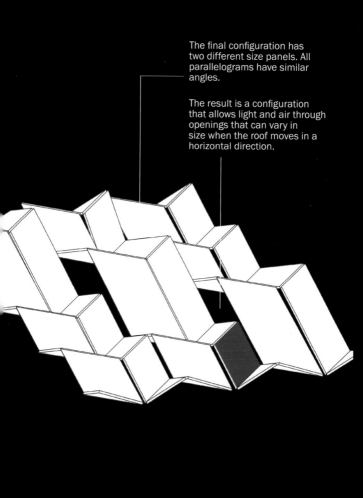

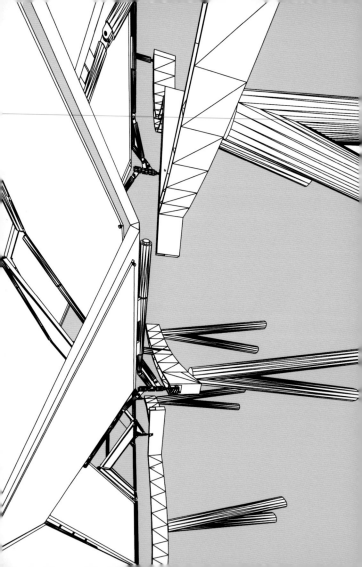

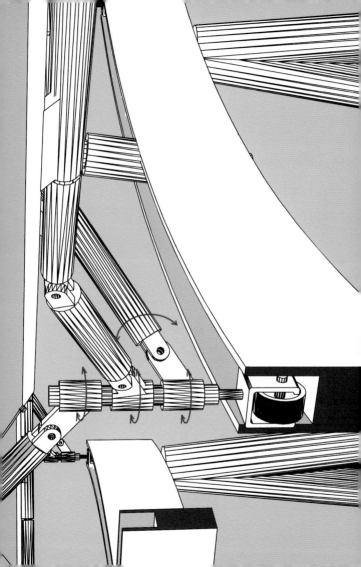

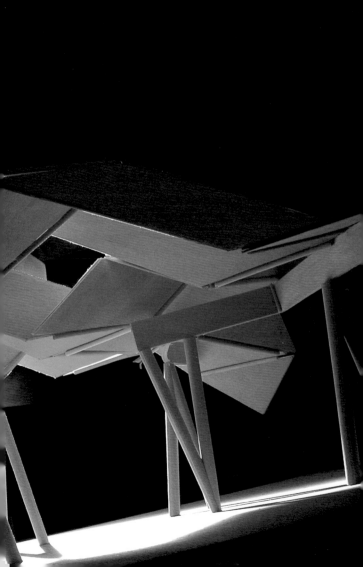

FAMILY *PONTEDERIACEAE*
Genus Eichhornia crassipes (Water Hyacinth)

Water hyacinths, otherwise known as *Eichhornia*, are floating aquatic plants. The petiole has an air-filled structure enabling it to float on water. Its roots are feathery and grow underwater. Air sacs are joined together as a group of floats to hold up the water hyacinth leaves for photosynthesis. A single air sac is unable to hold the leaf as it overturns in water.

Initial studies to establish a stable configuration for the air sacs involved filling up long plastic bags and balloons with air. The ends of the plastic bags were cut into strips to act as roots. When several plastic bags were tied together and placed on water, they were able to float. But when loaded, they became unstable, were easily displaced and toppled. A second study to arrange the bags in a pattern that could float and support load followed. The water hyacinth stays afloat with air sacs distributed throughout the plant attached to the base of the petiole, in a radiating pattern on plan.

In another study, balloons were used as hyacinth air sacs and arranged in various geometric configurations on water. It was discovered that triangular patterns were the minimum necessary to prevent overturning on load application. To simulate pneumatic floats, balloons were glued together standing on their ends as an optional stable configuration. The extent of the balloon below the water line would determine the usability and positioning of space beneath the water. After discovering a stable arrangement for the balloons to stay afloat whilst under load, floor decks with which to create usable floor area were configured to create a form of pontoon structure. A rigid hexagonal frame defined a platform with which to extend the usable area of the floats themselves.

The abstract analogue of the hyacinth was thus a series of three hexagonal platforms cantilevered from three inflated hulls, acting as primary floatation devices. The inflated hull could be made in PVC as a pneumatic structure and cable tied to ring beams acting as "collars" connecting hull to deck. A tensile roof fabric was selected as an appropriate structural form with which to define space over the hexagonal decks and curvilinear hull forms. The fabric was stretched over the masts and tensile forces were transferred via cable to hexagonal floor frames that connected back to three main ring beams each supported by a pneumatic hull.

Roof configurations were studied to provide enough cover and headroom over the hexagonal decks and the connecting sections in the centre of the three inflated hulls. The final roof form freed sufficient space required for movement between decks and maximised water views.

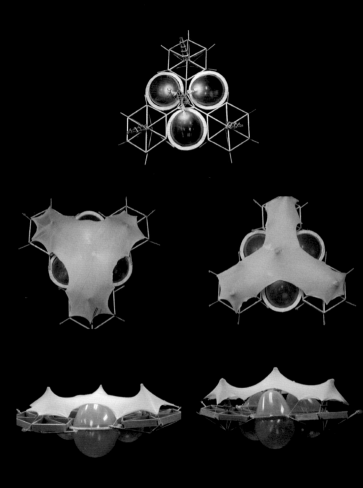

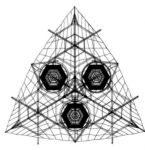

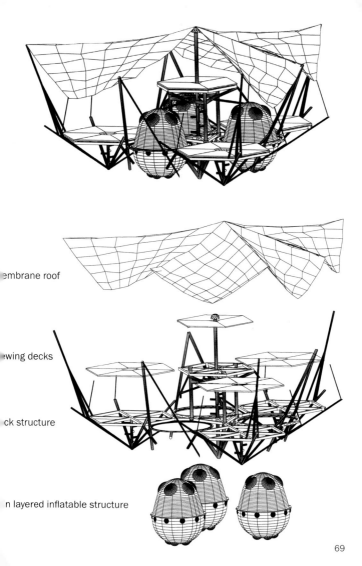

membrane roof

wing decks

deck structure

layered inflatable structure

69

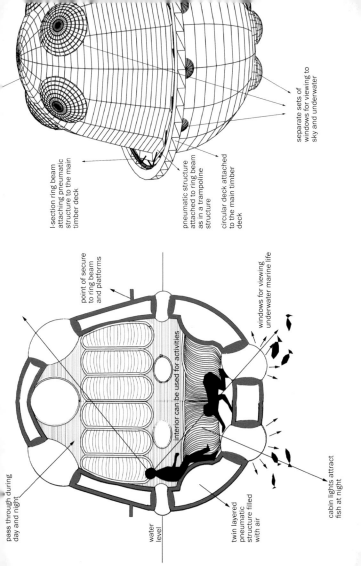

separate sets of
windows for viewing to
sky and underwater

I-section ring beam
attaching pneumatic
structure to the main
timber deck

pneumatic structure
attached to ring beam
as in a trampoline
structure

circular deck attached
to the main timber
deck

point of secure
to ring beam
and platforms

interior can be used for activities

windows for viewing
underwater marine life

pass through during
day and night

water
level

twin layered
pneumatic
structure filled
with air

cabin lights attract
fish at night

FAMILY *MALVACEAE*
Genus Hibiscus rosa-sinensis
(Hibiscus petal)

The petal layout of the *hibiscus* flower was studied in relation to its form and structure. The petals of the *hibiscus* flower overlap and rest on one another in order to hold up the entire flower. This supporting strategy occurs only in the lower half of the flower. The upper half spreads its petals out to attract insects and to provide a landing platform.

A study of the internal structure of a petal was carried out to determine the way the petal could stiffen itself given its surface form. Each petal had veins which converge and thicken towards the base but its stiffness achieved through folding its edges. Capillary tubes which branched from the veins, acted as braces for the veins. In the prototype, the main body was stiffened through triangulation of strut members connecting upper and lower chord members in a flat, undulating surface element. Edge members were folded upwards to stiffen the surface where it had the least structural depth.

In the first configuration model, the twisting of modules created an interesting shape but the forces of the load transfer were directed to the side of each module, hence making the petal module unsupportable. The final configuration saw petals linked in alternating directions, connected at the edges where they overlapped. This configuration allowed the forces of the load transfer to be directed to the petal end point.

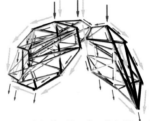

→ Actual load transfer path in this configuration
→ Desired load transfer path – the load transfer
pathway that was envisioned when the
"petal" was designed

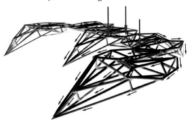

→ Actual and desired load transfer paths. The
loads were transferred from source to the
pointed base of each "petal" module

Original position of strut. It was later thickened to double its original thickness when deformation was observed.

Deformed strut position when force was applied in the direction of the red arrows.

Initially, only the struts indicated in blue were strengthened by increasing their thicknesses. This strengthened the connection between two modules. However, general twisting throughout the module and downward deflection were observed when load was applied on the blue members. Therefore, more struts (marked in yellow) of regular thicknesses were added as shown for both the 60m and 50m primary spans between supports. The addition eliminated general twisitng and minimised downward movements.

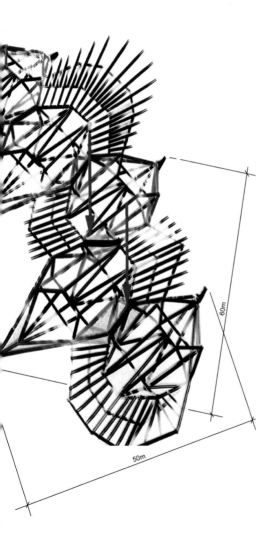

60m

50m

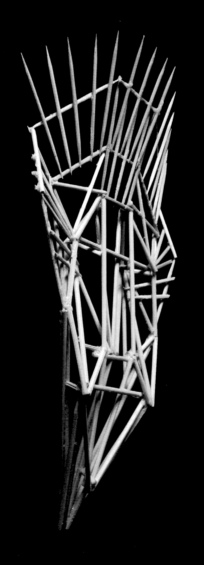

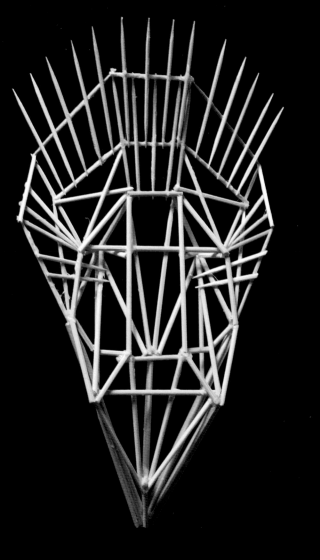

CENTRAL MODULE (50m span)   SIDE MODULE (50m span)

At 4kg,
no deformation

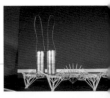

At 5kg,
no deformation

At 6kg,
no deformation

At 7kg,
first creak heard
but no deformation
observed. Load test
continued.

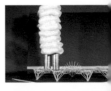

At 8.5kg,
creaks heard but
no deformation
observed. Load test
terminated.

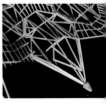

CORNER MODULE (cantilevered)

WEIGHT OF
MODULE:
225g

MAX LOADING
CAPACITY:
8.5kg

Ratio:
1:37:78

MIN LOADING
CAPACITY:
5kg

Ratio:
1:22:22

kg,
deformation

At 0kg,
no deformation

kg,
deformation

At 4kg,
downward sagging of
the corner module

kg,
t downward
ction
erved over
eral arch form

At 5kg,
excessive sagging and
multiple creaks. Load
test terminated.

kg,
k heard,
pparent
rmation.

At 4kg (with support),
corner module took on
load well. No sagging
or deformation.

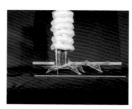

5kg,
ture failed.

At 7kg (with support),
two members
splintered but did not
fracture. Sagging
observed. Load test
terminated.

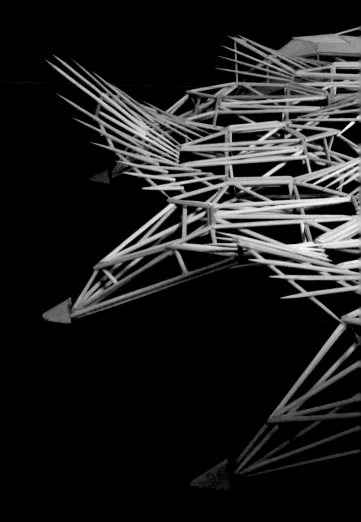

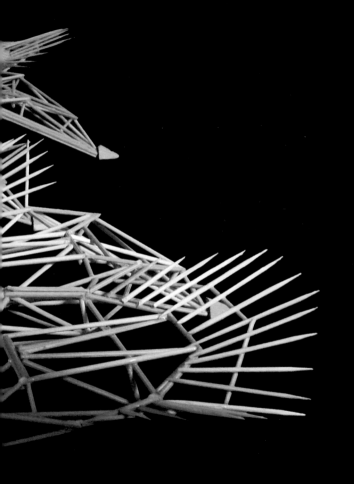

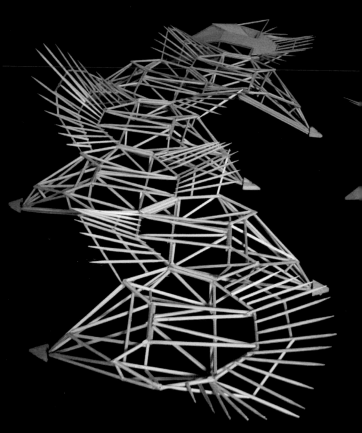

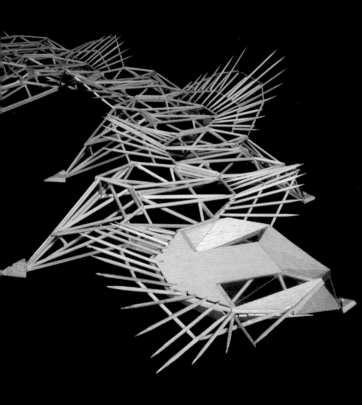

FAMILY *ASTERACEAE*
Genus Taraxacum officionale (Dandelion flower)

Each dandelion is made up of five fused petals forming a tube at the base and a single petal blade at the end. The tube is surrounded by numerous white hairs and contains the male and female components. The male component is made up of five free standing slender filaments that support a fused *anther* tube. The female component has a *style* extension that passes through the anther tube and ends with two pollen-receiving *stigmas*. The inflorescence is a collective composition of one to two hundred similar flowers, all bilaterally symmetrical and which has both male and female attributes.

Cross pollination is effected by the broad appeal of the dandelion and the timed sequence of blooming, but when cross pollination fails, the curling stigma lobes come in contact with the style to achieve self-pollination. Eventually the flowers wither and fall off leaving the hairs and seeds. The seed elongates while the hairs push against each other to achieve uniform seed distribution and maximum wind catchments, forming the familiar dandelion clock. The transition from a tiny bud to a full bloom dandelion clock suggests a modular structure that is first compact but expandable into a layered surface with multiple textures.

Various models were constructed in the search for a compact expandable structure. The collapsible sphere was made up of many three-legged units. The first prototype of these units had an inner structure that opened up at once. However, the dandelion undergoes many transformative stages from bud to fruit. To actualise this characteristic of the dandelion, the second prototype had an inner frame that cradles yet another frame which could unfold to a surface much larger than its base and cladded with a material different from that of the first layer. Each subsequent layer would unfold as the initial base approaches its maximum spread. The slight increase in the angle of spread at the base was magnified by a pivoting mechanism which then pushed the entire inner frame out and subsequently unfolded the inner frame.

This same principle was repeated on the innermost frame and in theory, more layers could be added to the prototype. Each layer of the prototype would expand at different rates such that a layer would be nearly full-open before the next layer opened. This could be used for devices that change functions and porosities at different moments in time, such as in the case of a solar panel or a rainwater collector. The prototype may also be a modular unit of a roof which can be combined to form larger spaces and collective functions by varying colour, texture, porosity and shape.

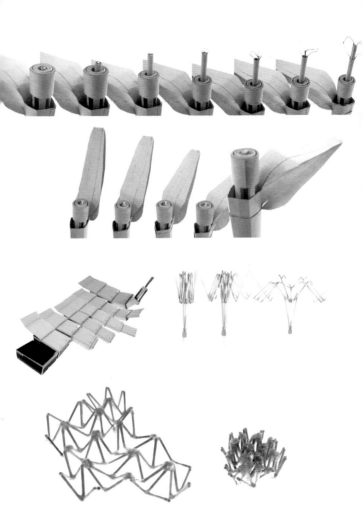

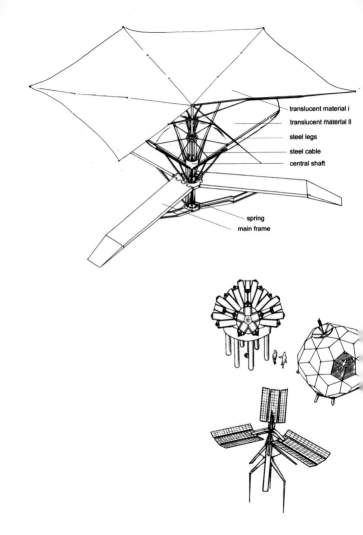

translucent material i
translucent material II
steel legs
steel cable
central shaft
spring
main frame

FAMILY *CARICACEAE*
Genus *Carica papaya* (Papaya leaf)

The biological function of the carica papaya leaf in attaining maximum exposure to sunlight without over shading each leaf, was used in this structural study as a prototype for roofs that controlled daylight and natural ventilation into the spaces it sheltered. A first attempt at combining one module of the abstract analogue was to interlock one another to form a self-supporting structure. However, the structure lacked rigidity due to a lack of continuity of supporting elements in transferring forces from one point of the composition to the ground plane. The basic hexagon was later identified and further developed as it seemed possible for the entire structure to become collapsible. Props were added to allow the structure to collapse in a swirling motion, translating the radial patterning of the petioles and the layering of leaves into a foldable structure. Flexible joints within hexagons enabled dynamic roof forms, and by connecting each hexagon to a central hexagon, the flexibility of the module could be manipulated on a larger scale. Two configurations for a foldable shelter were obtained by folding the hexagons into horizontal and vertical orientations. Joints were designed to allow multi-rotational movement required for both configurations, and a means to lock the rotating joints when the structure was set in place.

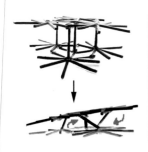

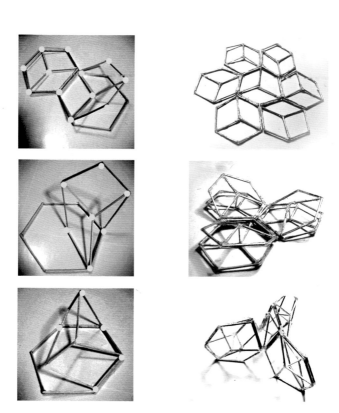

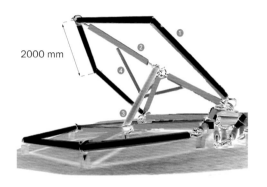

2000 mm

Foldable structure kit of parts:

1. 100 mm rigid aluminium frame

2. 100 mm tubular aluminium beam

3. 100 mm strut

4. 50 mm strut

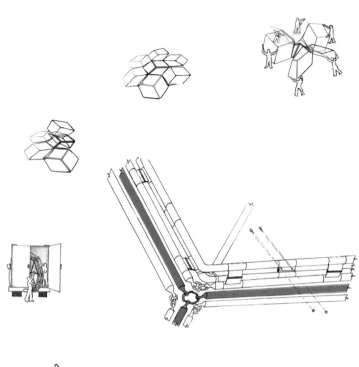

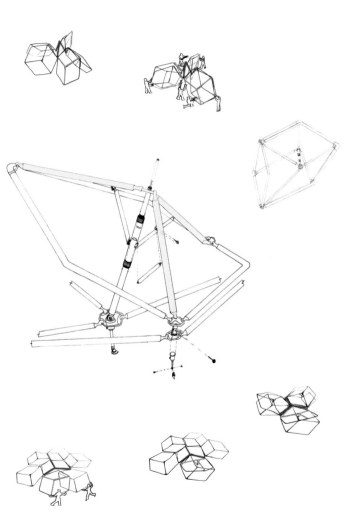

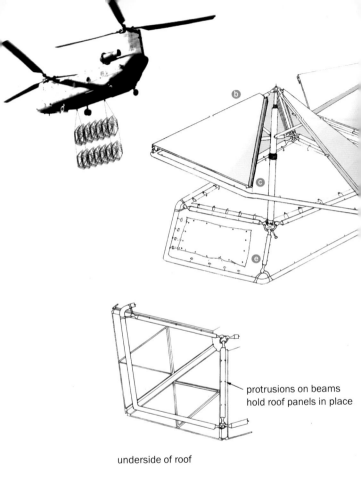

protrusions on beams hold roof panels in place

underside of roof

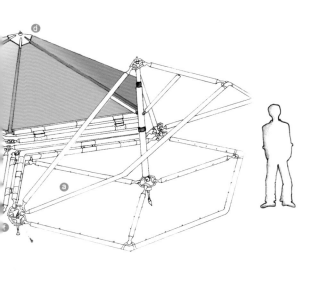

ⓐ 100mm diameter aluminium frames and beams

ⓑ polycarbonate roof

ⓒ 40mm wide gutter

ⓓ flashing

ⓔ string mat

ⓕ hydraulic jack with adjustable base to suit ground conditions

The first configuration for a foldable shelter was developed into a lightweight temporary shelter that could be used to house victims in the event of a disaster, transportable by land, sea or air. This configuration can accommodate 18 persons.

The second configuration was developed into a vertically oriented shelter with joints and struts in between each pair of hexagons acting as support for sleeping hammocks. This configuration can accommodate 12 persons.

g sleeping hammock

h loops on connectors to ease the hooking on and fastening of hammocks

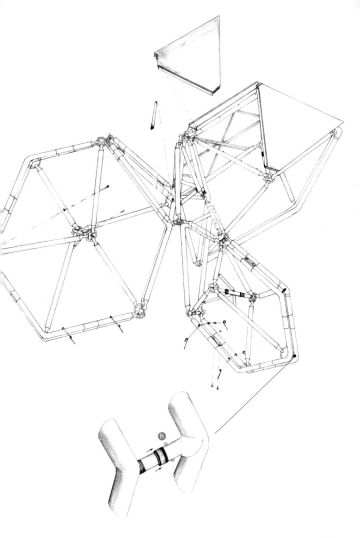

99

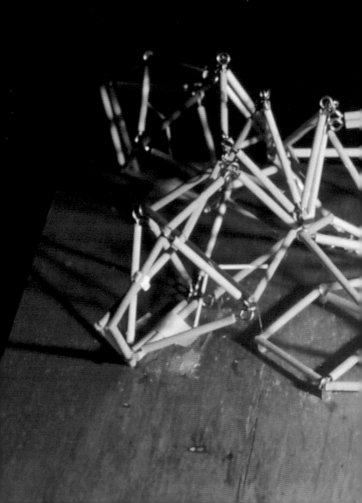

THE PEDAGOGICAL VALUE OF PLANT BIOMIMESIS

J.F.V. Vincent's biomimetic map of folding cellular plant structures attempts to chart the transfer of a biological idea into its structural application. Six biological aspects were identified as a basis for biomimesis, and correlated to the student projects in respect of folding structures, folding pattern, cellular growth, growth control, shape control and sensing.

In the folding canopy inspired by the hornbeam leaf, Vincent observes that unlike the radial actuation of the umbrella and its derivatives, a cover based on the leaf could be deployed and supported from a single extending strut.[1] In a radial leaf, experimentation shows that it can be actuated from a single fold. With the same hornbeam leaf, the student project however demonstrated the potential of asymmetrical folds actuated from a single point to cover a substantial area with simple supporting mechanisms. The student had created a surface which could unfold in two axes with openings perpendicular to its surface and configured a structural mechanism capable of transforming space through movement.

Vincent believes that in biomimetics, "the further down one moves from the natural origin, the more general and therefore, the more powerful the concept will be." The learning of structures in architecture through the biomimetic approach in the development of prototypes allows students to explore the relationship between force, form, and idea in generative modes of thinking crucial to design thinking.

In analysing engineering patents, Altshuller identifies levels of innovation which he listed as follows:

a single improvement to technical system requiring knowledge available within that system;

an improvement that includes the resolution of a technical contradiction requiring knowledge from a related area;

an improvement that includes the resolution of a contradiction at the level of physics requiring knowledge from other industries;

a new technology which involves a "breakthrough" solution requiring knowledge from different fields of science; and

discovery of a new phenomenon.

Altshuller believes that the analogical transfer of ideas from biology into architectural structures can be made at a variety of levels, depending on the remoteness of the technical problem from its biological model. If the remoteness is extreme, then a more basic analysis of the biological system is necessary in order to generate a useful paradigm. The biological basis of the studio projects is useful at the conceptual level of generating a rich variety of potential structural solutions in architecture, whilst allowing students to explore different levels of innovation in their individual processes to the best of their individual activities.[2]

Notes
1. Julian F.V. Vincent, "Deployable Structures in Nature", Deployable Structures (ed. S. Pelligrino) (Springer, Vienna)
2. G. Altshuller, Creativity as an Exact Science (Gordon & Breach, New York, 1988); G. Altshuller, And Suddenly the Inventor Appeared (Technical Innovation Center, Inc., Massachusetts, 2001)

ANIMAL ANALOGUES

The study of biological sciences by military technologies focuses on issues of camouflage, detection and sensing, locomotion (over extreme terrains) and the flight of miniaturised objects for surveillance purposes. Steven Wax argues that the biological mechanisms of self-protection, self-propelling, self-fuelling, self-healing and adaptation to dynamic environments form the ideal characteristics sought in defence systems and are the subject of military research.[1]

Carnegie Melon University's Sensor Based Planning Laboratory investigates energy effective forms of locomotion in species of snakes and fish as potential forms of terrestrial movement. Effectiveness is measured in terms of metabolic cost incurred in resolving undulatory forces generated by the creature's body and the ground/water reactions for propulsion and navigation. The School of Engineering (Aerospace and Mechanical Engineering) of the University of Southern California researches into the winged flight mechanisms of small creatures for application into small airborne objects.

Apart from research on competition sailplanes, aerodynamics research has only focussed on larger aircraft which fly at faster speeds. The low speed flight of miniaturised objects are more complex and although their forms are unfettered by high speed aerodynamics, other issues of stability, manoeuvrability and wing span to body ratios and locomotive mechanisms set in. Geoff Spedding and John McArthur's research have developed a means to analyse lift and drag forces of small curved wings and the spatial gradients of the airflow, originally thought to be difficult quantities to estimate.[2] In this sense, zoological aero and hydrodynamics can inform small-scale aerodynamics as one approach to analysing the forces which act on the small scale flying object. Current electromechanical (and other) technology enables engines to overcome flight propulsion and stabilising issues without a limit to form.

What is the relevance to studies in architecture and structure?
It is not the technology that is holding engineers back from building the plan but it's the design – what it would look like. It would look like a dragonfly, a moth, a bat, a bird or none of the above.

Spedding's comments mirror the situation in architecture; there exists a gap between the objective and the subjective in which designers operate. Energy and building efficiencies are subject to requirements of space, usage, mechanical and building quality although their designs are based on ideals and standards of resource conservation in the context of building systems shells and skins in specific climatic and cultural contexts.[3]

The question arises in a design studio attempting the study of structures in exploring architecture: How can we operate intrinsically spatial term to craft a structure in ways which do not begin with the subjective values of building function and efficiency? If the natural forms we study have intrinsic efficiencies which determine and are determined by their morphological and biological systems, then how do we interpret these intrinsics in architecture?

Wax argued that whereas understanding nature is necessary, it is not sufficient to accomplish (design tasks at hand) and that traditional engineering approaches can execute the effects of nature without mimicking form and system. (Nature's devices and materials surpass those of human artifice). Instead one possibility was to derive analogues from the natural system to create a working principle for a structural/spatial prototype.

In Otto's experimentations with tensile structure, his flexible column prototype captured the essence of the vertebrae spine where the profile of the column was dependent on the varying degrees of tension applied to the wires at the base of the study model. This same system enables the human back to bend. The idea was further explored by Jane Werrick, in Marks and Barfield's Bridge of the Future, in the structure of their quadruped spinal "bridge". Like the spinal cord in the vertebrate column, the pedestrian deck was supported by tension elements and protected by Y-shaped compression elements held in position by prestressed steel tendons. Constructionally, it was designed as a propped cantilever system as the erection sequence moved from one support to the opposite side.

Movement in space-saving architecture is explored by Hoberman in his prototypical investigations which form the basis of future developments in portable shelters, stadium roofs and kinetic structures.[4] Michael Fox experiments with responsive systems integrated with the building envelope in his kinetic structures lab.

The following projects explore moving mechanisms in animals to articulate patterns of movement which were capable of transforming space and shelter with structural form and envelope.

FAMILY *TESTUDINIDAE*
Tortoise

The unfolding frame is a structural and formal abstraction of a tortoise, but is not derived from the skeletal structure of the animal. The recoiling action of the tortoise into and out of its shell is the characteristic movement captured in an abstract box frame. There is a "mother frame" which accommodates parts of spatial enclosures and which extends from the frame. The initial model has a single element unfolding from a mother frame. The final model develops multiple elements which unfold from the main frame, translated as balconies, decks and moveable screen walls of varying porosity. The proportions and composition of this frame are determined by the parts and vice versa, and which transform space at various stages of recoils and extension.

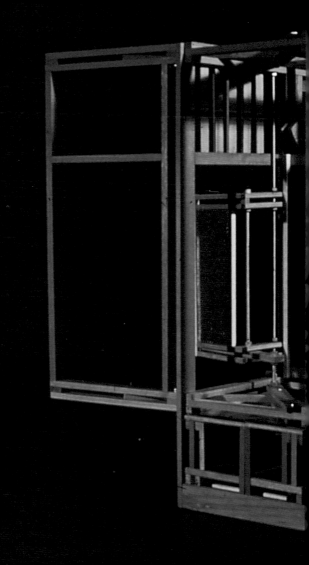

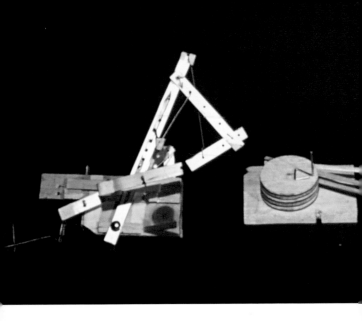

FAMILY *ARANEIDE*
Spider

Early models illustrate preliminary attempts at capturing the spider's movement with two-dimensional mechanisms. These were effecting movement on a single plane, was later developed into a space enclosing configuration comprising hinged legs pin-jointed at two locations. The structural prototype effected movement in a direction perpendicular to the plane in which the hinged legs (of the spider) flared out.

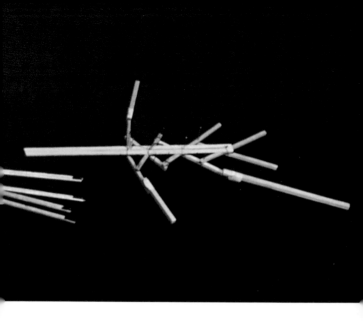

This structural prototype is a mechanical translation of the spiders movement using wires and hinged struts configured in a way which uses rotational motion applied to a central "thorax" to change its overall form. It has implications on the design of roof shelters when modified into a cable stayed roof with its tension members operable by winches capable of extending roof arms effectively.

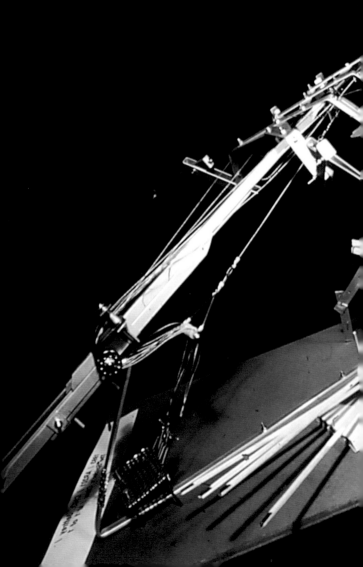

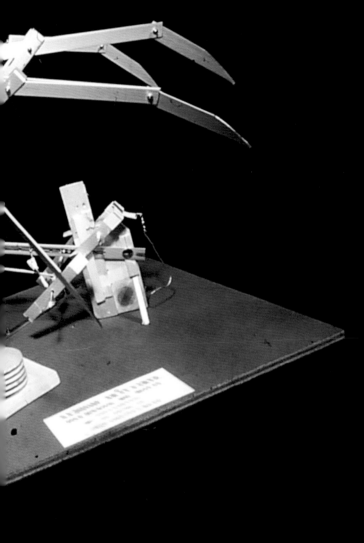

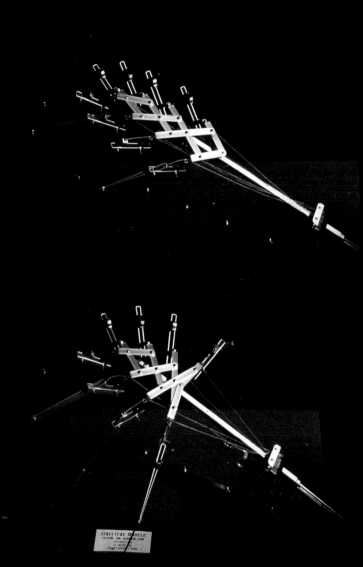

STRUCTURE MODULE
TUTOR: DR. JOHN W. LIM

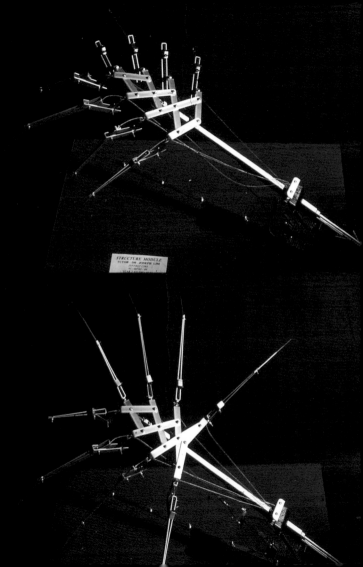

STRUCTURE MODULE
TUTOR: DR JOSEPH LIM

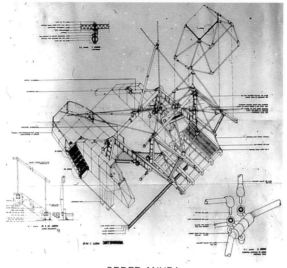

ORDER *ANURA*
Frog

The mechanism is based on the frog's leap which is characterised in a movement where it rears back and leaps forward in one smooth sequence. The movement is adapted into two stages of extension, and applied as alternative positions of a sheltered observation deck. The supporting elements are proportioned according to structural span, to points of support and to supporting hierarchy. The initial translation of the frog's leap attempted by the student involved the movement of a small element along a thick wire bent into an arched profile. Subsequent studies involved the development of extension in the element itself to represent the leap. The device for effecting extension involved an adaptation of a collapsible mechanism, reacting against a hinged anchor. The roof canopy structural frame was to enable two positions synchronous with the deck positions and detailed as a discrete element supported off the inclined moveable struts.

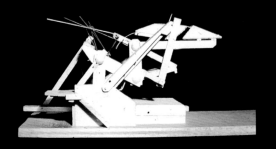

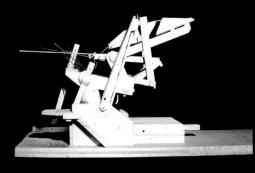

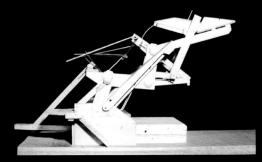

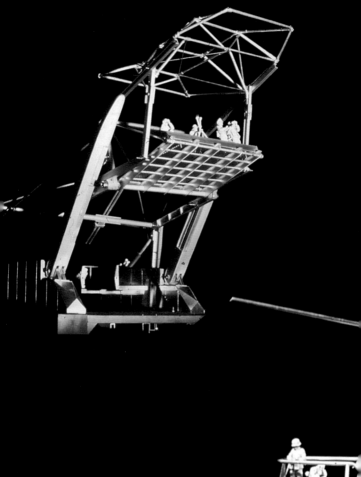

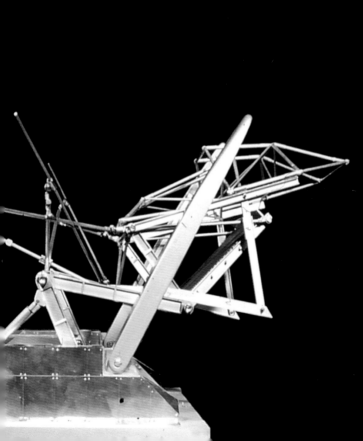

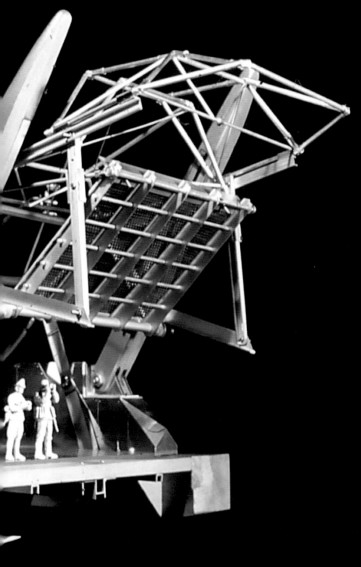

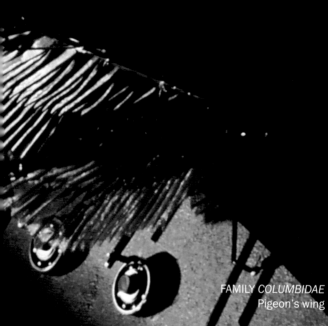

FAMILY *COLUMBIDAE*
Pigeon's wing

The structural analogue is extracted from two aspects of a pigeon's wing in flight: the material action of the flight muscles; and the positions of the wing in one cycle of motion extracted from movement in flight. The mechanical analogue of flight is constructed out of a metal model using ball-bearing and umbrella struts as the supporting structure. The struts are rotated by connection to the ball-bearings, 'moving' the wire mesh wings assembled in different starting positions of the wings. The wings are pleated for rigidity assuming the wing positions of the pigeon as it flies, and their positions in space are varied by using ball-bearing housings of different diameters.

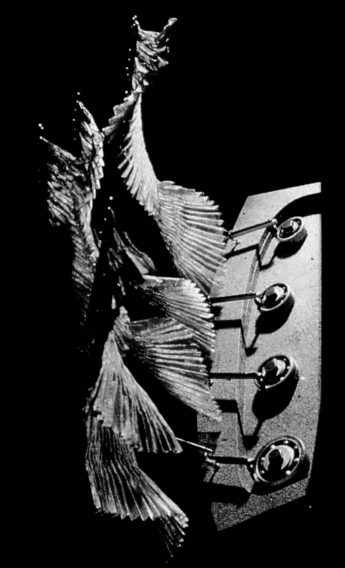

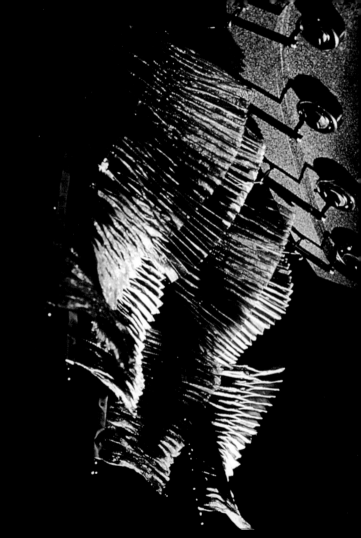

FAMILY *CHIROPTERA*
Bat's wing

This is a scheme based on the structure of a bat's wing. Essentially, the bat's wing comprises skin stretched across bone tissue, and its form varies according to the particular activities in which the bat is engaged. For example, the wing forms a cape, wrapping around the body of the animal when it is asleep. The wing also extends in flight, and based on this idea, the student sets out to capture the framing mechanism which allows a membrane to vary its shape. Shape is varied by changing the positions of fixed supports, which are varied in the metal struts. Changing the positions of the ends of the supporting frame changes the forces through the structure, thereby changing the form of the entire object. It is perhaps one interpretation of Engel's funicular structure.

Three degrees of movement are possible with this model: the main stem which can be anchored at any point on the wire grid; the pin-jointed umbrella struts which are equivalent to the mammalian digits; and the wires running along the wing tips which allow the digits to extend or contract. The exercise is a conceptual study into how force changes form.

FAMILY *COLEOPTERA*
Beetle's wing

The beetle's wing folds up when it is not flying and was an idea which generated the formal hierarchy of the parts of the animal. Here, the mechanical analogue bore no resemblance to the biological structure of the animal but instead characterised its kinetic movement.

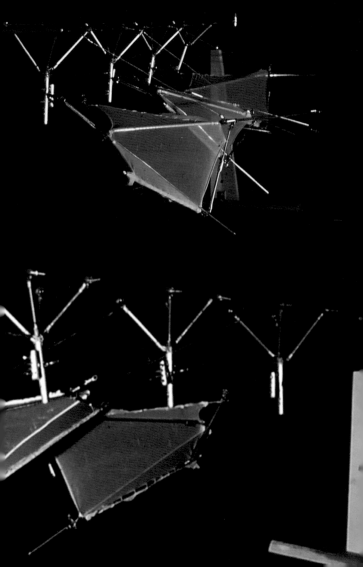

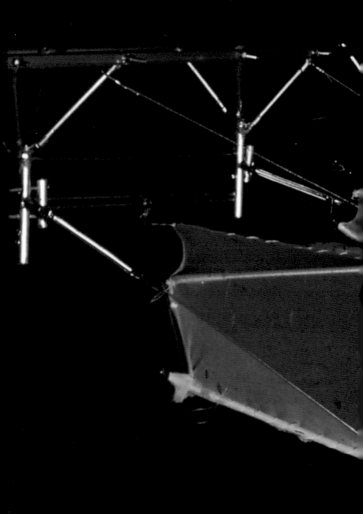

FAMILY *CAELIFERA*
Grasshopper

Three ideas generated the development of structural form: the hierarchical relationships between the parts of the grasshopper; the conception of space within this hierarchical relationship and the order in which the insect moves its legs.

Initial study models indicated the extraction of three components to the structural form: wings (roof), body (deck) and legs (supporting columns). These were developed from an intermediate collage necessary to assist the students in visualising form as a whole. The segmentation of the body is captured in the articulated seating modules attached to one side of the bridge body. The structure was to be a pavilion in a natural landscape. The wings were strutted in a pattern sympathetic to the main lines emanating from the entire composition. The columns supported both wings and legs and were reduced to a minimum number of three. Three columns metaphorically expressed the insect using only sets of three legs to move at one time. Space occurs between the wings and the body and a secondary deck below the main body.

In this example, the structural abstraction was visual. The compositional hierarchy of form was based on this meaning which subsequently determines technical considerations. Prior to arriving at the structural prototype, the process was likened to a technical production of an abstract idea, i.e. the mechanical essence. The form or "pre-form" was made out of a framework of structural elements, all performing a specific function and reduced to a minimum necessary to shape the form and to enable movement. The design of the form in its parts as elements to a structural whole was considered with the development of the joint-type and the motor devices to effect mechanical movement and to locate the position of pin joints. The design process oscillates between the technical and the abstract, in relating considerations of structure and architecture.

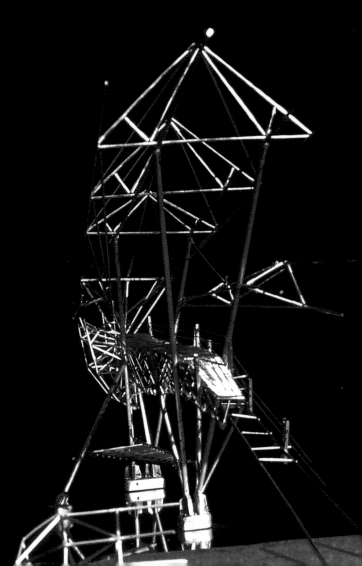

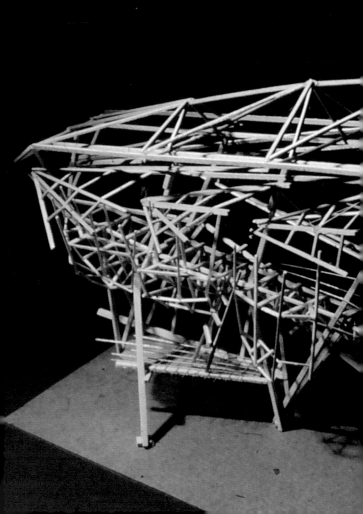

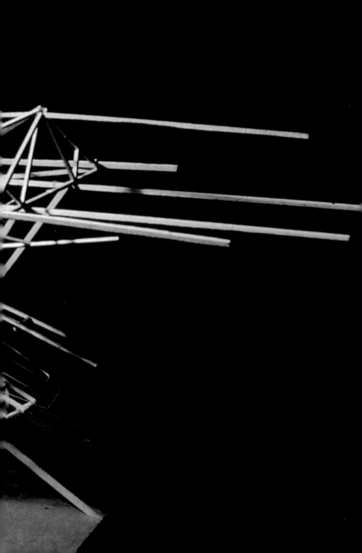

CRITICAL SUMMARY

In the study of locomotive systems in nature, the bio-structural analogues were adapted into space-changing devices. To do this, specific programs were required for the analogue to respond to considerations of culture, light, space, shelter, support and ventilation; in order to shape its development into a prototype. At this stage of the design process, a few variants of the analogue surfaced from the design exercise.

Analogues could function in specific ways which characterise the animal studied without visual resemblance to the animal. For example, the unfolding cuboid frame means the tortoise recoiling into its shell, but does not resemble the tortoise in form or in structural (shell) system.

Analogues may resemble the animal studied in visual form but does not represent its structural system. However, the kinetic analogues would move in a way which characterises the animal. This is the case of the analogue based on the frog.

Analogues may visually resemble and behave structurally in ways similar to the animal studied.

The study of movement in relation to structure and form allows the integration of abstract and tangible elements of kinesis in the architectural program. Bio-structural analogues allow the development and generation of alternative solutions to shelter and space-changing enclosures by referring to the mechanical aspects of form-structure relationships derived from examples in nature. The formal tectonics was a result of function and construction based on the mechanism enabling movement. This took on various paths:

the skeletal system of the animal and its structural action in enabling movement is applied to a space-modifying prototype; and

the structural prototype was not based on the locomotive system in nature but captured its characteristic movement, as in the case of the frog and the tortoise.

These exercises relate kinetic force to form through the study of joint-types and lever-action (first, second and third class levers) in connection with the design of structural elements. The design ideas can be generated from the mechanism, and the latter becomes the schematic template for further development of structure and architecture.

Notes
1. Steven G. Wax, Exploiting Nature through Materials and Design, Defense Sciences Office, USA
2. Geoff Spedding, Professor in Aerospace and Mechanical Engineering; John McArthur, Graduate student in Aerospace and Mechanical Engineering
3. Cultural and political aspirations often have little to do with resource conservation at the point of building but thereafter, they have been sustainable through time and do not generate energy debts in their operation.
4. A.D. Profile No. 102, Folding in Architecture

CORAL ANALOGUES

In some species of coral, their structural morphology is likened to the Gothic fan vault patterns of Grodecki where thickened ribs articulate lines of force in a three-dimensional spatial configuration transmitting load from vault to columns.[1] In both the Gothic precedent and the corallite structure, the structures comprise freely bundled tubes acting as columns.

The corallite or polyp skeleton is complex in structure, and is a tube with vertical plates radiating from its centre. The plates are septo-costae which stiffen the tube in each growth cycle, growing in alternative orders in between each other. Horizontal plates (coenosteums) connect tubes together and the wall comprises three skeletal elements which vary in proportion in different coral families.

The radial elements of the corallite are divided by the wall into septa (inside the wall) and costae (outside). Costae seldom extend beyond the wall, except in corallites that do not project much above the surrounding skeleton. In these cases, the costae join one corallite to the next.

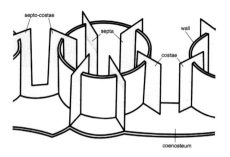

Skeletal elements
Diagrammatic representation of the basic
skeletal elements of a coral

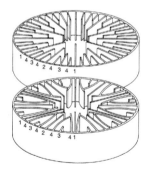

Septa
Numbers indicate cycles

Corallites sharing common walls but do not form valleys are called meandroid, and those which formed valleys are called cerioid. The structural names of each coral describe their distinctive growth forms, for example corals which form valleys without common walls are called flabello-meandroid.

The colony development of coral species has allowed them to be free of several limitations of the solitary individual.[2] Corals form colonies by a budding process which involves two sets of polyps, the parent polyp and the daughter polyp which forms on the side of the parent. Colony growth forms depend on the type of the budding in some corals, but are completely independent of it in others. There are colonies that exhibit other types of formation.

Other modes of colony formation are described by shape rather than by structure. Massive (similar in all dimensions), encrusting (forming a layer on to the substrate), columnar (column forms), branching arborescent (tree-like), foliaceous (leaf-like) and laminar (plate-like). Complex structures exist in any colony, which are variable in shape, size and design to adapt to differing environments in entire reefs. These developments have occurred within species giving many species a wide range of growth-form options, each suited to a different set of environmental conditions.

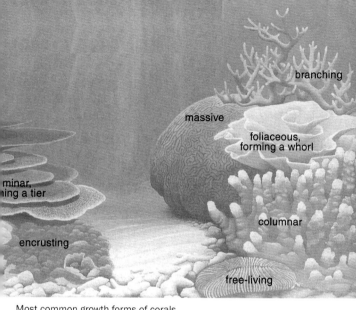

Most common growth forms of corals

Eight morphological corallite characteristics are used to classify and distinguish different coral species:

Calice : cup-shaped depression on the corallite surface
Coenosteum : skeleton between corallites within a colony
Columella : central axial structure (vertical rod) within a corallite
Corallite : skeleton of an individual polyp, solitary or within a colony
Costa(e) : extension of septum beyond the wall
Dissepiment : horizontal partition (flat or curved) within or outside of corallite
Septum(a) : radially arranged vertical partitions within a corallite
Wall : vertical structure enclosing a corallite

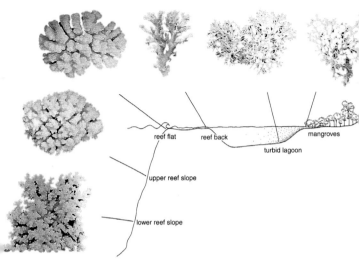

Variation in the skeletal structure of colonies of *Pocillopora damicornis* from a wide range of habitats at a single geographic location

GROWTH FORM

Variations in the growth form of corals are in response to sedimentation, growing space, water temperature, availability of the food nutrients, the force of sea waves and the degree of natural light exposure relative to their position on the reef slope. Corals on the upper slope are small but solidly constructed. Down slope where wave action is less severe, coral colonies are larger and have less bulky skeletons with greater variations in form. Light availability and water turbidity also affect growth and form responses. The most delicate coral skeletons are found in turbid lagoons or near mangrove edges. Corals also have the capacity to modify their growth form in response to the activity of neighbouring corals and even polyps of the same colony with different micro environments, over large areas. Forms can mutate to overgrow neighbouring colonies within genetic limits.

In an extension of Ernst Haeckel's radiolaria coral drawing of 1862 which inspired the imagination of generations of engineering designers, the form of other coral skeletal structures are useful subjects of study and provide a basis for studying strength through structural pattern.

The following series of projects were based on studies of corals in the investigation of spatial-structural prototypes in an attempt to explore alternatives to Euclidian and Cartesian models of form and space.

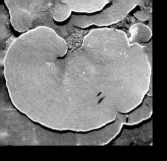

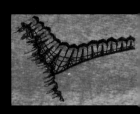

FAMILY *AGARICIIDAE*
Genus *Pachyseris*

Pachyseris species have horizontal or sloping folia that are thin and delicate. The septa are arranged in parallel directions which give their upper surfaces an appearance of closely packed ridges and valleys, both of which are concentric and parallel to the corallum edge. Septo-costae are very fine and tightly compacted. The skeletal structure of this foliaceous reef coral is of mechanical and ecological significance. The skeletal material is elastic and brittle in a linear direction relative to its cantilever growth form. Whereas the entire skeleton is configured for stiffness, its strength varies with anatomic direction. The organisation of the structure is imposed by a directional growth of the septo-costae which determine the directional strength of the coral configuration. Skeletogenic tissue acts as shock absorbers from the constant flexing in tide surge. The way the skeletal configuration of the coral determines its strength and resistance to fracture, forms the basis of the mechanical analogue for the prototype. A flexible cantilever anchored to one end as opposed

to a rigid cantilever; given its proportion of span. The idea of flexural strength to resist tide surge in the coral is translated to a moving mechanism in the cantilever structure where rows of septo-costae are sandwiched between. The decision to employ a tension system has two chief advantages. First, the flexural strength of the large cantilever may be maintained by varying the intensity of the tension force in the set of cables. This allows a range of curvatures possible in the structure (which can be appropriated to change the spatial profile beneath it). Second, the septo-costae plates may be further articulated as moveable elements in the mechanical analogue which vary the porosity of the surface structure as a light mediating envelope. The abstract drawings indicate sectorial distributions or corallite material before septo-costae articulation and its rationalisation as a tensile structure which can change its configuration according to the degree of force secured at its anchor.

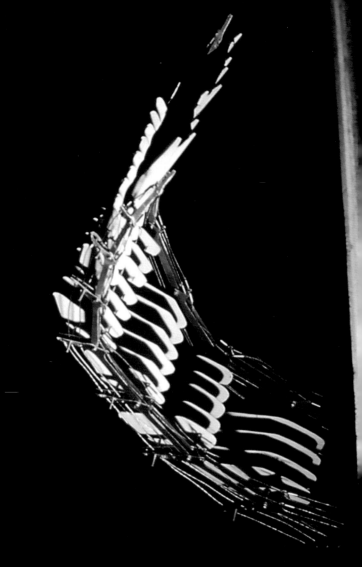

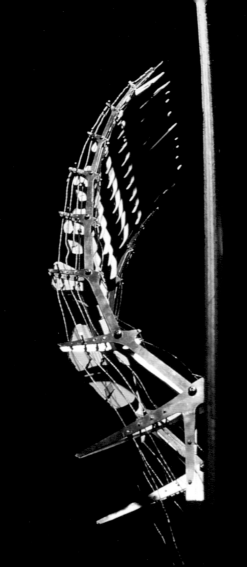

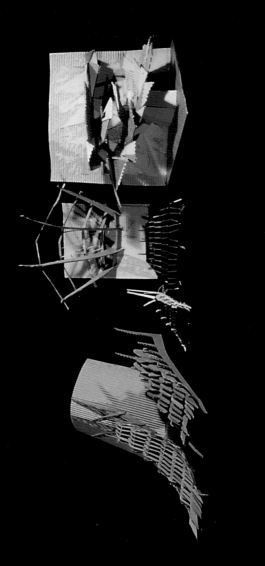

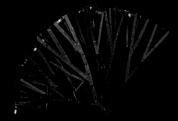

FAMILY *MUSSIDAE*
Genus *Isophyllastrea rigida*

The *isophyllastrea* species have a cerioid colony form, massive as in boulder like. Its corallites bud intranaturally and its columella are trabecular. Corallites of the *isophyllia* are joined in longitudinal series to give a district pattern of ridges and valleys, the latter being elongated, Y-shaped or irregular. The spines of *isophyllastrea* are large and sharply pointed on the septal margins and the columella is formed by a mass of interlocking spines. The abstract model of the corallite began with coarsely proportioned plates bundled in a manner similar to the trabeculated columella. The initial study models attempted a pattern of the budding polyps in multiples of two to four and 16. This configuration was eventually modified to a tree-like structural analogue capturing the sectional profit of the coral skeleton intersecting at the uppermost portions of the branches to form the interlocking spines. The structural action is in compression, where the intersecting struts reduce the buckling length of the linear elements composed as a series of vaulted roofs, enclosing wave-like spaces. The intersecting struts create a form of lateral bracing to the entire modulated structure.

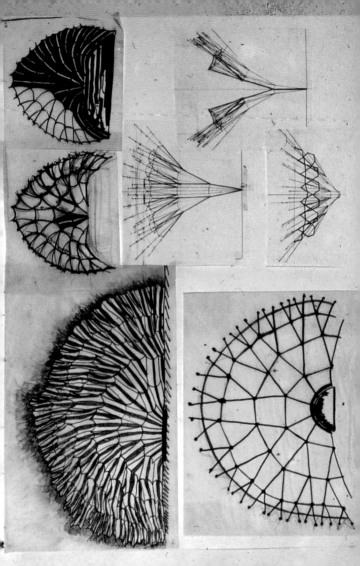

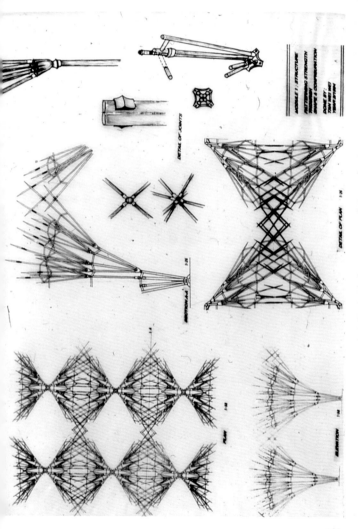

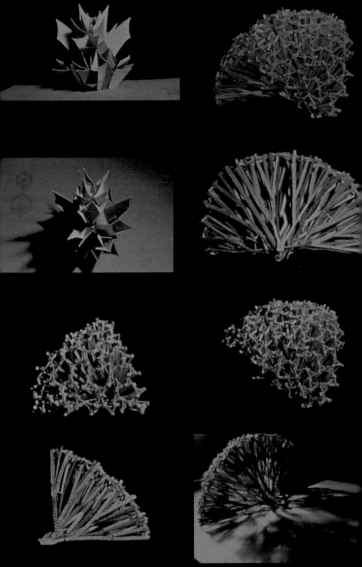

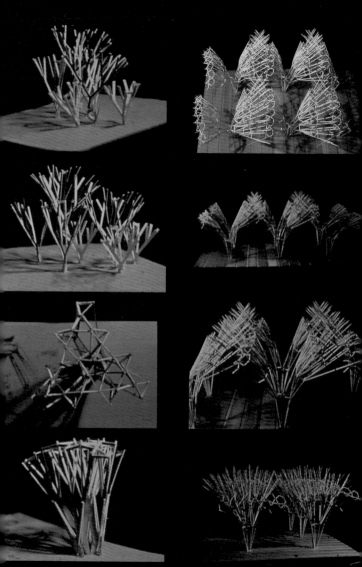

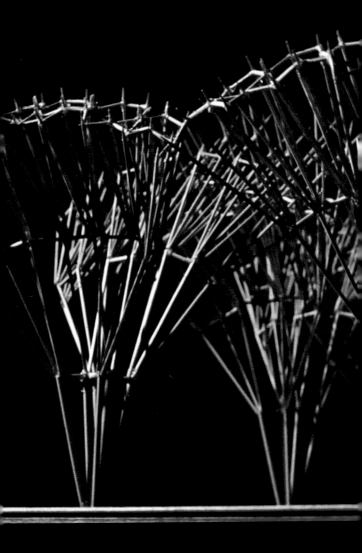

CLASS *ANTHOZA* (extinct corals)
Rugosa

Rugosa or *rugose* corals (referring to their wrinkled appearance) are also known as *horn* corals. Solitary *rugosans* are horn-shaped whilst colonial types have hexagonal corallites. Solitary *rugose* corals are a few millimetres in diameter and length to 14 centimetres in diameter and one metre in height. Colonies can be four metres in diameter. The coral animal feeds itself using tentacles to capture and sweep organisms into their mouth, when situated in intertidal rock pools. *Rugose* corals have radial septa stronger than their transverse platforms. Both major and minor septa radiate from the centre. *Rugose* corals have bilateral symmetry with new septa growing in alternate insertion patterns between older ones to maintain a rigid structure. As the corallite

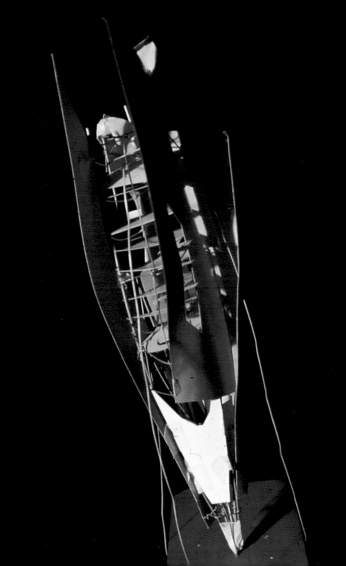

grows, the septa spread further apart and new septa are added, usually four septa at a time to maintain a rigid structure. The general trend among *rugose* corals was to evolve a strong skeleton. Several different lineages demonstrated convergent trends toward similar morphologies, for example, carinae and columella were developed to strengthen the septa and the central axis of the coral as it grew. A columella is a column grown through the middle of a corallite by thickening the end of the counter septum. This natural characteristic of the *rugosa* coral was translated into an analogue which attempted a structural tube that carried an outer layer of septa. At some points, the septa were fused into the tube. Alternative septa material were used to explore translucency with stiffness and strength, and the effect of a structural skin fused with the structural tube.

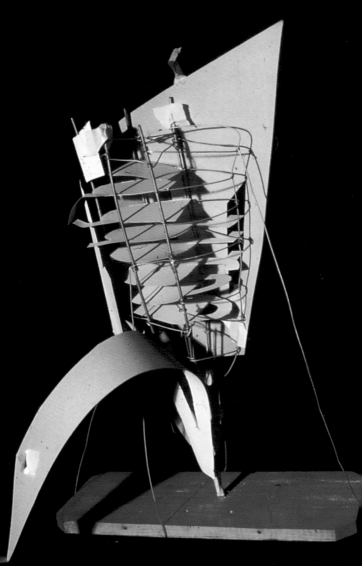

FAMILY *DENDROPHYLLIDAE*
Genus *Tubastrea*

Tubastrea form low-growing clumps of corallites that arise from a common base. Its polyps are sometimes extended during the day but at night, the corallum is hidden by a ring of bright yellow tentacles. Corallites are well separated, cylindrical or turbinate and is characterised by the fleshy living tissue which obscure the smaller septa. The skeleton of the *tubastrea* is porous created by numerous septa arranged in cycles. Costae are present as low ridges. The focus of the *tubastrea* characteristic is in the recoiling and extending tentacles, integral with the corallite-skeleton. This analogue attempts a structural tube that can recoil and extend in one axis in a diagonally arranged collapsible structure with unfolding "tentacles" in the end. This study enables one structure to change shape on plan and in section with a simple pin-jointed mechanism to transform the length of its tube-like structure in one axis. The idea of "transformable space frames" in this context enables different volumes of space within expandable enclosures acting as an integral structure. This prototype is a significant departure from the idea of a building as a primary structure carrying fixed floor plates and a separate skin acting as spatial enclosures. Instead, it explores the idea of a transformable structural tube capable of changing its interior space proportions.

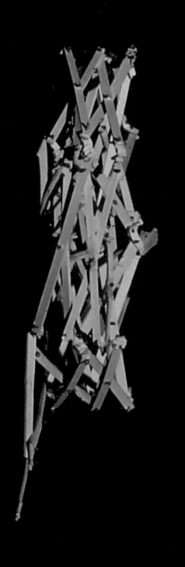

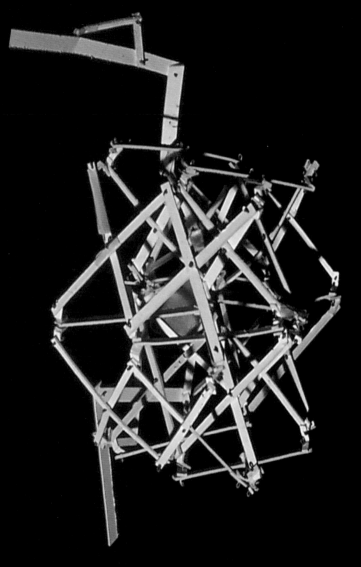

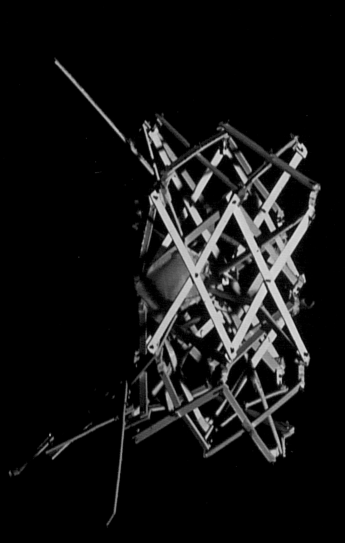

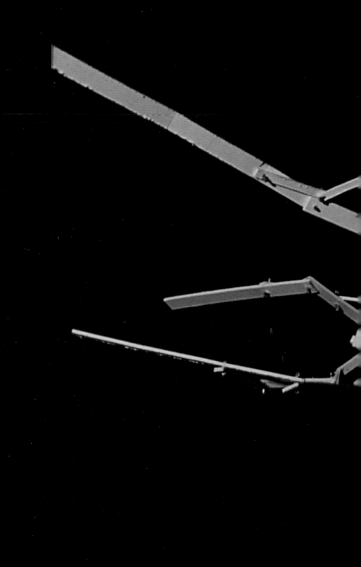

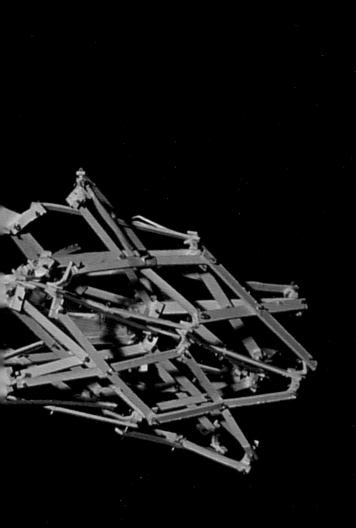

FAMILY *MERULINIDAE*
Genus Hydnophora exesa

The *hydnophora* have branched or massive colonies with noticeable corallite centres. The skeletal structures are faviid-like but are highly fused without paliform lobes. The valleys often become obscured as they spread like a fan. The septa are finely dentate and closely packed. Here, the student translated the conical form into an isolated tessellated dome acting as a surface structure with the upper portion forming a strutted and folded cantilever assuming the fan-like configuration of the valleys between corallites. The surface folds of the structural analogue increase the rigidity of the spatial module that is hydnophobic in character. The translucent material at the upper part of the analogue suggests light filtering possibilities, for an outer canopy to an inner space enclosed by the domical component of the structure. The sculptural study of the cantilever is structural and composed congruently with the domical element. There is a propensity for the analogue to be developed as a surface structure or as a triangulated space structure.

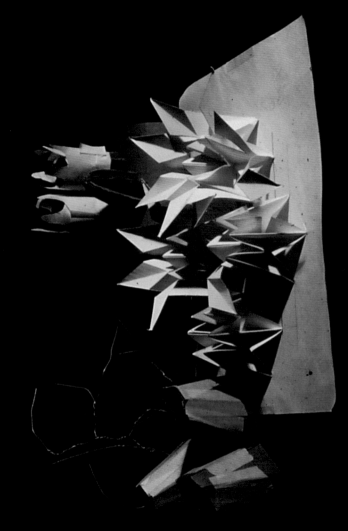

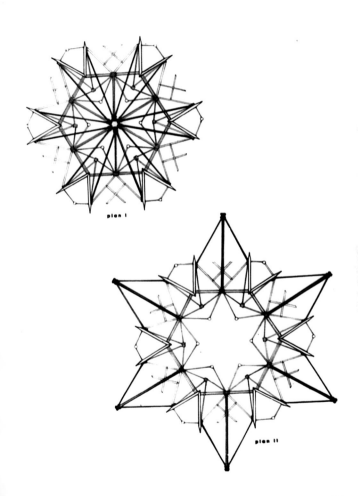

plan I

plan II

183

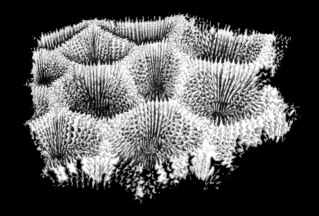

FAMILY *AULOPORIDAE*
Genus *Bayhaium*

Genus Bayhaium is characterised as a *cerioid syringoporinae* coral with well defined mature and immature regions. The mature portion of the corallite is thick-walled, septate, and normal to the surface of the corallum. The immature portion of the corallite is thin-walled, non-septate and inclined with respect to the axis and surface of the corallum. Corallum is massive, ramose and dominantly cerioid. The corallites are prismatic in the cerioid portion of corallum and cylindrical in restricted phaceloid areas of its outermost mature portion. Walls are separate and composed of a single layer of prismatic crystals normal to the wall, greatly thickened by septal sclerenchyme in the mature region. Septa are represented by 18 to 24 sclerenchymal ridges, septal ridges coalesce forming alternating layers of thick and thin wall structure in mature portion of corallum. There are irregularly spaced, tunnel-like connections between corallites. There is no axial structure or axial tube in this species.

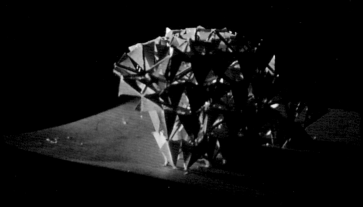

In the structural study, idea of septal ridges coalescing to form alternate layers of corallum structure is translated into a trihedral module forming successive layers in a hexagonal grid plan. The structural analogue acts as a space frame with triangulated compression struts capable of carrying load several times its weight. The model illustrated carried four fully loaded carousels before failing at its weaker points. The structure allows for layers of space in between non-load bearing planar screens which can be framed by the trihedral structure. Diaphanous screens were explored to reduce the weight of the overall structure. The prototype may be configured as a diaphragm wall or as a free standing structure, with openings for shelter, shade, ventilation and natural lighting. Polyhedral kites were configured to catch air with the lightest yet stiffest frame which maximised fabric area for catching wind.

FAMILY *MEANDRINIDAE*
Genus Ctenella chagius

The *ctenella chagius* coral structure appears as a series of walls and valleys due to the incomplete separation of their individual polyps. In colonial scleractinians, the individual polyps are no longer visible, having fused into long, meandering rows that resemble the wrinkles of a human brain. Local skeletons are made of calcium carbonate secreted by polyps as aragonite. The type of skeleton is determined by the balance between the processes of calcification and the extension of the coral's tissues. The tissue of the *ctenella chagius* coral extends very slowly while laying down calcium carbonate at a fairly constant rate, so its skeleton grows very dense. On closer inspection of the walls and valleys, there are ridges with a small gap between the tentacles, hidden in the tiny grooves on the sides of the ridges for protection. The polyps use their tiny tentacles to feed on animals and particles from the water around them. Some tentacles are armed with nematocysts (stinging darts) which paralyse their prey (such as tiny shrimp) before they are moved into the mouth cavity. The polyps absorb food and pass nutrients

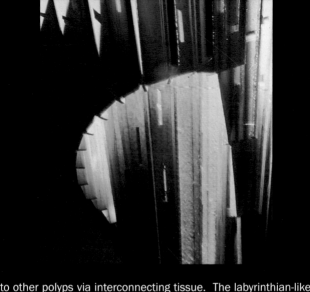

to other polyps via interconnecting tissue. The labyrinthian-like structure of the coral with its ridges and cavities are captured as walled layers forming cellular compartments in the study model. The inner whorls of walls are configured as structural diaphragms where the transverse plates strut two innermost facing walls. The transverse plates which are on the outermost walls act as buttresses to increase the surface area of the structural material forming the labyrinthian cavities. The structural configuration of the analogue allows for minimal thickness whilst achieving stiffness and strength in directions perpendicular and planar to the whorls. Transverse plates are required to be as long as the walls they strut, and continuous in length in order to maximise their stiffening effect on the entire configuration. Perforations in the transverse plates are kept to a minimum so as not to weaken them when acting as a diaphragm or buttress.

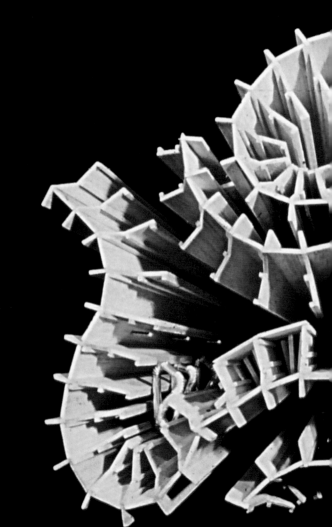

CRITICAL SUMMARY

The biological features of the coral species significant to these studies in structure and space were meaningful in many ways.

Different species used a generic morphology in assuming different forms of existence (as individuals and as colonies, in shallow or deep water lighting conditions) by mutating elements of their septa and theca, in order to adapt to varying substrate topography and the quality of food environments.

These morphological variations between cerioid colony species offered strategic differences in structural analogues ranging from vaulted compression structures to modular units with space frame action, creating unique spatial characteristics.

Other studies such as the *pachyseris* coral lead to a cantilever drawbridge mechanism capable of varying curvature with relative degrees of force in its tension and compression members. This could be applied to an enclosing element capable of changing space with changing curvature.

Yet the *ctenella chagius* coral's abstraction illustrated the possibility of a multi-layered curvilinear cellular entity acting in compression and bending, strengthened by diaphragm action, a form which is easily associated with cellular plans.

Most remarkable were the *tubastrea* studies, in particular the transformable tube structure which could vary its proportions relative to x, y and z axes. This enabled a change in its enclosed spaces, allowing for intermediate stages of change and their respective spatial proportions.

Notes
1. Louis Grodecki, Gothic Architecture (New York, Rizzoli, 1985)
2. Jen Veron, Corals of the World Volume 1 (Australian Institute of Marine Science, 2000)

    *Coral species images, coral structure and growth form illustrations are copyright of Dr JEN Veron and Australian Institute of Marine Science * Image of rugosa coral is the 29th plate from Ernst Haeckel's Kunstformen der Natur (1904)*

SEASHELL ANALOGUES

The studio began with a primer on the nature of seashells beginning with the classification system used in conchology. Molluscs are categorised according to principal features such as their shape and surface morphology, and their feeding, respiratory, reproductive and growth systems. Of specific interest to the studio was the fact that mollusc shells grow accretively with minute calcium carbonate deposits placed in patterns and at thicknesses to achieve maximum shell strength and rigidity. Folds, ribs, and spirals, which resist both internal and external forces, serve to strengthen the shell's structure along its surface. These structural strategies gave the students clues as to how their designs could be strengthened in subsequent stages of "prototype" development in the studio exercise. In a second primer, students studied the theory of surface structures in order to understand the form-strength relationships in buildings. The students then explored the similarities in the structural action of building surface structures and those in natural seashells whilst also noting their differences.

In addition to the study of shell structure and growth, students also were attentive to biological mechanisms that enable the movement of various parts of the organism. Students saw that these mechanisms – by virtue of their ability to regulate porosity to light, water and air, or to protect the animal from harsh environmental elements -- had the potential to be translated into other architectural features, such as the enclosure of a building. Moving parts of the organism were also analogous to flexible building components, which might allow for programmatic flexibility.

In the first phase of the studio, students were asked to select one type of shell for study on an individual basis. They each identified a significant geometric pattern in the shell structure that might reveal the resistance of compressive forces.

Some students also looked for a biological characteristic of a mollusc entailing mechanical action or movement. The students then created an abstract analogue in the form of a structural model that related space and form to load or movement, as derived from each of their seashells. These structural models specifically explored abstract geometries relating architectural form to seashell characteristics in a provisional way. In abstracting an analogue from the natural form of the seashells, the studio projects searched for a connection between pattern and structural action in seashells related to the overall configuration of the seashell and the folding patterns on the shell surface.

In the second phase, subsequent developmental models were developed and tested for structural and mechanical action and for the ability of these properties to change and to qualify space. Using live loads, each model was tested to its carrying capacity before buckling. Attributes of the model (for example, the direction of folds in relation to the direction of forces) could then be modified and re-tested for improved strength. These developmental models eventually led to prototypes or architectural elements that would have the potential – outside the immediate aims of the studio -- to be incorporated into a real site and a real program.

Students selected five classes of seashells in the taxonomy of molluscs: *Gastropods*, single shell creatures; *Bivalves*, double shell creatures; *Polyplacophora*, shells made of segmented plates; *Cephalopods*, spiral shells with internal chambers and *Scaphopods*, tusk shaped shells.[1]

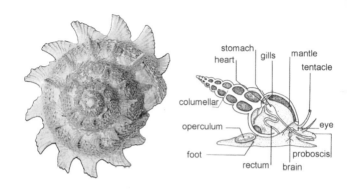

Labels: stomach, heart, gills, mantle, tentacle, columellar, operculum, eye, foot, proboscis, rectum, brain

CLASS *GASTROPODA*

Gastropods comprise 75% of the world's molluscs with half the species being marine. Most *gastropods* are highly mobile creatures with small eyes, tentacles, mantle and a broad flat foot. The gills, stomach and heart of the creature are contained in a singular, coiled hard-shell. The shell grows in a spire along one axis in all variations of this class.

Genus Astraea heliotropium (Sunburst Star Turban)

The sunburst star shell has the form of a flattened spire with a distinct ornamentation in its structure; the cantilever 'starburst' protrusion acts as a transverse stiffener along its spiral form. In the abstract analogical model, the façade is an unravelling of the spiral with intermittent ribs transverse to the line of material growth. In the study process, the student began with curved surface elements, and then proceeded to identify lines and

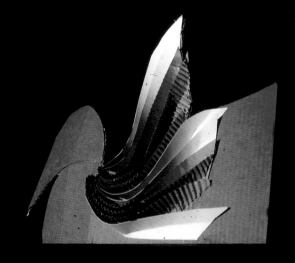

edges in an interim model before developing late-like folds to stiffen the free-standing "wall." The steeper the individual folds, the more stable the folded wall. The test model demonstrated the possibility of sculpting screen elements around openings for light and ventilation. In both the natural shell structure and the prototype, material action is translated in the longitudinal and transverse directions. The façade had to be stable in two axes whilst supporting the roof elements cantilevering to one side of the screen. The cantilevers are made more rigid by folding in order to cantilever "further" from the finger-like shell. The student varied the proportions a, b, c in the sectional profile of the façade to overcome the moment created by one-sided cantilevers. The last prototype illustrated is a hybrid of two types of rigid surface structure; the curvilinear fold of the roof element acts as a cantilevered transverse shell structure whereas the angular pleated folds of the screen element provides the benefit of a folded plate structure.

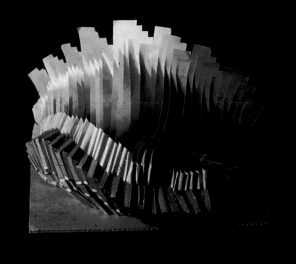
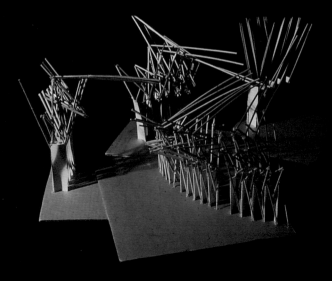

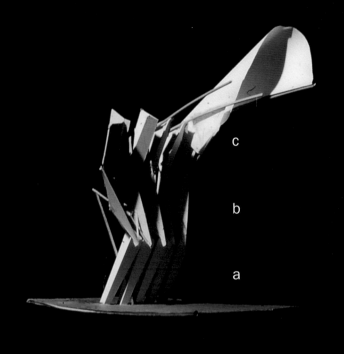

c

b

a

Genus Busycon sinistrum
(Lightning Whelk)

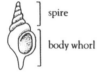

spire

body whorl

The shell of the Lightning Whelk has an elongated spiral along one axis with intermittent thickenings along the axis transverse to the spiral. These thickenings form pointy ridges, giving the shell its name. The transition of the ridged spine into the opening of its large whorl is seamless in the lightning whelk. One student translated this juncture into an analogical model whereby the flatter, wider "roof" panels transform congruously into the deeper, thicker support elements through a triangulated and ribbed surface pattern. In the transverse direction, the folds provide the sectional depth required of the arching action to transmit compressive forces along the surface and edges of the structure. The triangulation is intensified at the "base" of the arch structure when the surface transforms from roof "plates" to Y-shaped columns. In the longitudinal direction, load is transferred by the continuous triangulated pattern of the roof to the same Y-shaped supports in a 3-way grid. The ridges in the shell spine were developed as ridges and valleys in a surface structure made out of non-equilateral panels folded for rigidity. The folds enable the surface to resist loads in both transverse and longitudinal direction.

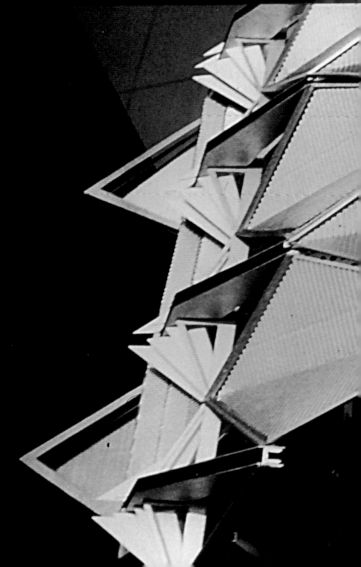

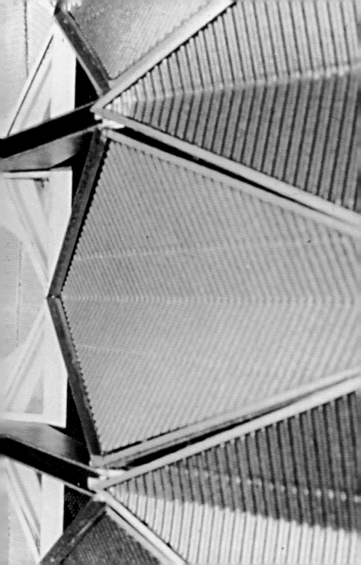

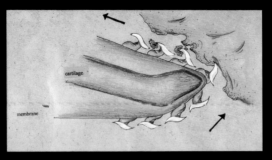

Gastropod Radular

Most *gastropods* carry a retractable organ, a ribbon of chitin called radula which bears rows of rasping "teeth". The mollusc gathers its food by rasping against vegetable, plant matter or flesh. The moving structure developed in this scheme was based on the feeding mechanism of the mollusc. It was developed as an element which changed space and the quality of light filtering through its structure. This is possible with a hinged frame rotating about a fixed support frame. Both "layers" of the enclosure lift up to become an integrated roof and ceiling element. The radular elements can change their position to affect the pattern and intensity of natural light falling into the interior space. Here, space is transformed physically and changes in character through the quality of light mediated by structural elements. The structure could be adapted to different degrees of porosity as an enclosure by changing its "radular" profiles. The degree of interchangeability of the prototype to accommodate specific and different functions was explored in the structural elements which were developed as a combination of mainframes and accessory cladding systems.

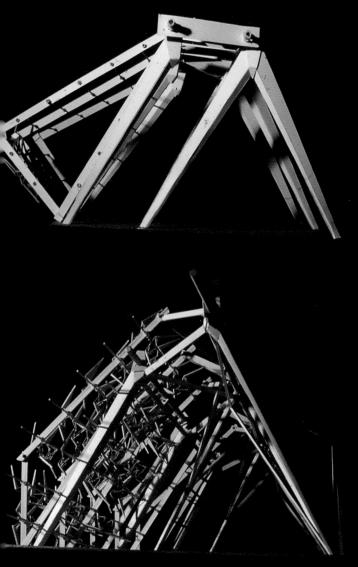

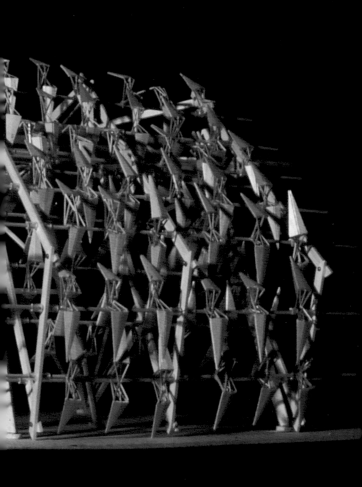

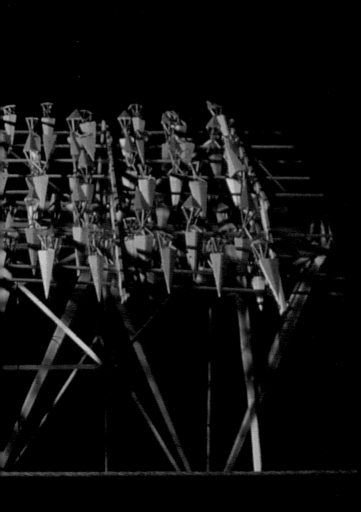

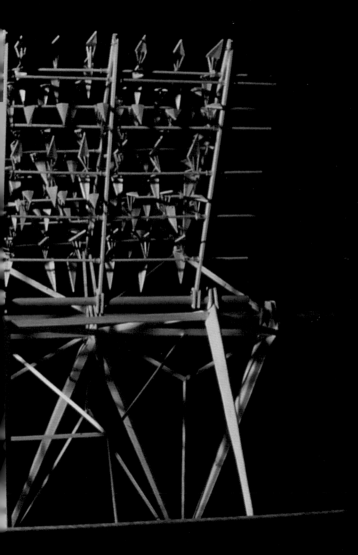

CLASS *BIVALVA*

The *bivalve* shell comprises two halves that are constructed in layers laid down by the mantle, the mollusc's outer skin. A special secretion called conchiolin is secreted from the mantle which catalyses the hardening of calcium carbonate into material for making the shell. *Bivalve* shells are classified according to their teeth and hinge structures that join the two shells together. The shapes of valves vary considerably and different species are capable of burrowing and creeping over substrate, whilst others fix themselves in one place. Some swim by forcing water contained within the shell through a jet at the rear edge, or by clapping their valves, in a "bellows" fashion (scallops).

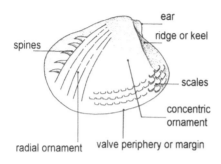

ear
ridge or keel
spines
scales
concentric
ornament
radial ornament
valve periphery or margin

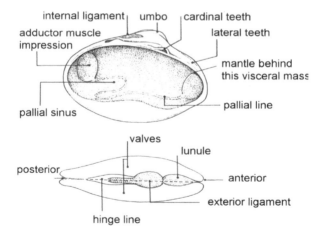

internal ligament | umbo | cardinal teeth
adductor muscle
impression
lateral teeth
mantle behind
this visceral mass
pallial sinus
pallial line

valves
lunule
posterior
anterior
exterior ligament
hinge line

In the fluted clam, the radial ornament and the spines are most developed in the external valve. These external features are defence mechanisms to prevent predators from getting a firm grip of the mollusc, and to withstand water pressure at greater depths. In the initial study model, the forces (and materials) intersect in an opposing pattern. This pattern enables the fluting of the form for structural advantage and for the natural extension of light scoops, as cantilevers from the two way grid radiating from support points. The final prototype found resolution in a two-pin segmented arched vault. The resultant form compensated for its low rise to span ratio; the structural depth of the arched vault segments increased when folded. Moreover, the two symmetrical forms acted in exact opposition mutually cancelling unwanted bending moments. This prototype combined two salient aspects of the fluted clamshell: the interlocking diagonal arrangement of its calcium tissue and the fluted surface form of the shell. Also, the protruding roof elements had the potential to incorporate light scoops in alternating directions richly folded to achieve surface action in load transfer. A frame model was first used to clarify fold direction and intersection points. Subsequent models transformed (thick) frame into (thin) ribs with the addition of structural infill to achieve surface action.

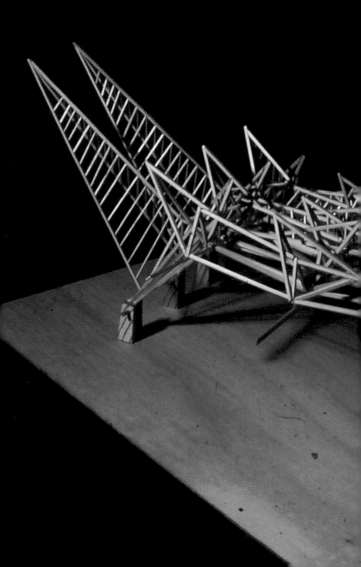

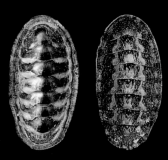

CLASS *POLYPLACOPHORA*

The *polyplacophora* class are primitive molluscs possessing flexible shells that comprise eight segmented plates held together by a girdle, allowing the animal to tightly coil itself in defence.

Genus Tonicella lineate (Chiton Mollusc)

In the *polyplacophora* class are examples from the *Chitonidae* family commonly known as chitons or "coat of mail" shells (chitons resemble woodlice). The curvature of its entire body is changeable by contracting the girdle along its outer rim. This causes its component shells to slide over each another when propelling itself in the water. In the example illustrated, the student translated the chiton segment plates into a cardboard model of sliding pieces over a shallow arched curvature. The entire assembly, which could only slide, was not rigid in any position once it moved, and could not support live loads. The scheme explored the ability of a surface element to expand in

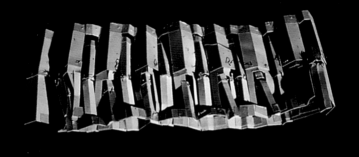

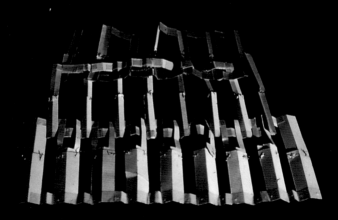

one or two directions in an arching action. The ability of the prototype to maintain its load bearing ability in different curvatures emulates the essential quality of the chiton shell, which in nature is an elegant and complex system of segmented plates held together by a versatile "girdle." This girdle acts as a ligament connecting the segmented plates together, performing as a hinge and roller, capable of acting both in compression and in tension when necessary.

Another student attempted the translation of both sliding and arching movements of the chiton girdle with hinged compression elements in a two-way grid supported on a parallel grid. The compression elements of the vault could vary its curvature by changing its support positions in two horizontal directions (see a, b) on tracks. Both prototypes generated may be used as roofs, ceilings or 'wall' elements and both possess the ability to accommodate a limited range of floor plans. To improve the load-bearing capacity of the model, the cardboard material was folded in a two-way prismatic pattern to create a vault with structural arch action. The vault could be "shortened" in length by placing the supports closer, a movement translated from the sliding plates of the chiton.

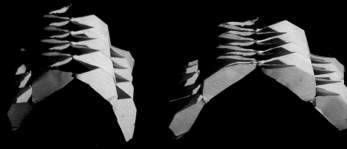

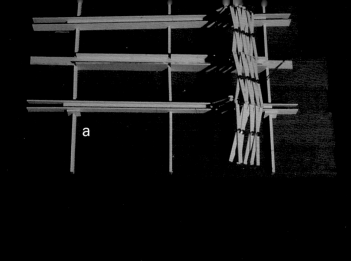

a

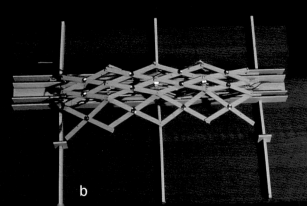

b

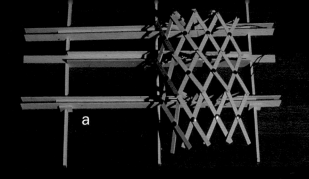

a

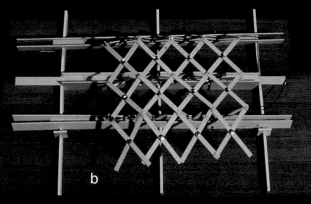

b

CLASS CEPHALOPODA

Cephalopods are a relatively small group of highly mobile and carnivorous molluscs that possess tentacles with suckers, powerful beak-like mouths and large eyes. Although this class includes squid and octopus, the *Nautilidae* family, which has an external shell, is referred to in this project.

Genus Nautilus pompilius (Nautilus Shell)

The nautilus shell generated a study in two opposite kinds of spaces: the successive diminution of tiny chambers, and the open-ended space that an infinite coil implies. The *cephalopod* is the chambered nautilus which is a large spiral shell, subdivided into sealed compartments each smaller than the preceding one. Since *cephalopods* are free-swimming shellfish, mobile and carnivorous, the compartments act as submarine ballast tanks for the creature to vary its buoyancy in water. With the aid of a siphuncle (a central tube connecting all chambers), the nautilus is able to pass varying amounts of nitrogenous gas and fluid to rise or submerge at will. The nautilus shell, like most seashells, combines the advantages of both transverse and longitudinal

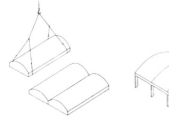

transverse shell   longitudinal shell   doubly curved shell

shells. Shells of double curvature allow for more favourable distribution of internal forces. In the case of the prototype based on the nautilus shell, the intersection of doubly curved 'vaults' was intended to stabilise the composition.[2] The free ends, however, needed to be stiffened by a system of tied-arches in order to maintain stability. The compartmentalised chambers of the nautilus shell were expressed in the final prototype as a series of doubly curved intersecting vaults with a sub-chamber in each main vault. These arched intersections intercepted the compressive forces from the vaulted surface and transmit those forces to the supporting points. The surface structure was continuous and assumed a form that, although asymmetrical, was structurally stable in both directions. The wire mesh was a representation of a lattice structure that indicated the direction of forces from roof to supports. The model was able to withstand a compressive load many times its weight, failing only when the thin upright columns buckled. If the wires overlapped in tighter multidirectional grids and the supports were better configured against buckling, its load capacity would have been improved. This example illustrated a structural form that was inseparable from the space it defines.

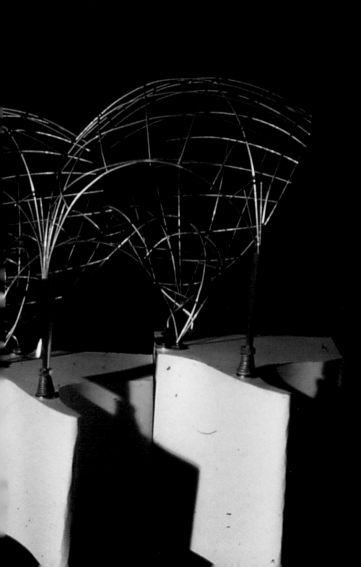

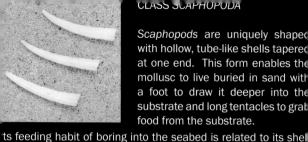

CLASS SCAPHOPODA

Scaphopods are uniquely shaped with hollow, tube-like shells tapered at one end. This form enables the mollusc to live buried in sand with a foot to draw it deeper into the substrate and long tentacles to grab food from the substrate.

Its feeding habit of boring into the seabed is related to its shell architecture which is shaped as a tusk to enable it penetrating the seabed.

Genus Dentalium elephantinum (Elephant Tusk Shell)

The analogy of 'drawing sustenance' from the sea was matched with the kelong function. (A kelong is an offshore structure used by Asian fishermen to catch fish with large nets supported by wooden poles driven into the seabed).The shell modules shine light onto the trapped fish at night when harvesting. They are luminaries and accommodate working platforms. *Scaphopods* have longitudinal flutings in their shell architecture to take compressive forces at either end, and to resist bending along the length of its body. Doubly curved shells were developed by Felix Candela in the late 50s which could be composed of straight line elements. This simplified the preparation of construction formwork. In this prototype, simple timber sections were used to form a lamellar shell. The closer the net of straight lines, the better the approximation to the curves of a hyperbolic paraboloid. In the Kelong structure, the rattan (cane) shells were arched over rhombic plan areas and tilted, creating an asymmetrical pair of hyperbolic paraboloids. The double curvature of the shell enabled a balance of internal forces which required only very small material thickness to stiffen the surface.

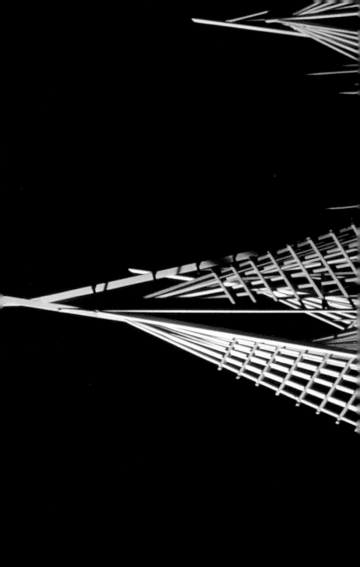

THE PEDAGOGICAL VALUE OF STRUCTURAL CURVES AND FOLDS

The curvature of most shell forms in two axes, is effective in resisting bending and compressive forces generated by predators and water pressure. In the case of the bivalves, the sectional profile is thicker near the hinges from which the leading edge of the bivalve grows forward as a structural cantilever. The leading edges of larger bivalves are also folded (as in the case of the clam) with radial and longitudinal ribs to further strengthen the shell. This prevents fracture in the thinnest part of the shell by compressive forces. Where the folds of the seashell are thinnest, the entire surface coils to compensate for the 'lack' of material (and material strength) at that part of the shell. For very thin edges, 'r', which is the radius of gyration referring to the girth of compression members affected by buckling, is increased in the overall configuration by folding (Figure 1).

Angerer postulates that thin surfaces can only sustain bending forces to a limited extent when stresses act perpendicularly to the plane of the surface. Therefore, typically in shell construction, such stresses are avoided by curving the surface so that stresses now act within the plane of the surface. With folded structures, this is achieved by folding where surface panels are inclined towards the main forces acting along the ridges and valleys of the fold. Sharp angles in the folds give greater stiffening effect to the structure. Both structural types are suitable as lightweight roof elements but the formwork for folded structures is easier to construct than curving forms.

In the case of the *Chiton*, *Lightning Whelk* and *Fluted Clam*, the students conceived the sharp-angled, prototype structures as folded frames (Figure 2).[3] The *Chiton* folds were designed in such a way that individual part surfaces met in exact geometric

Figure 1

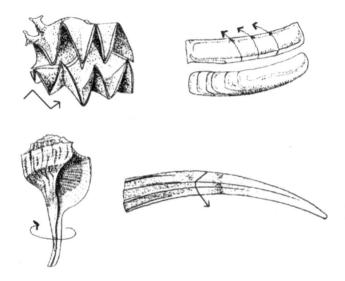

Figure 2

Figure 3

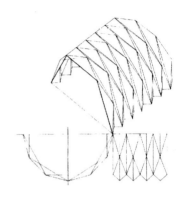

relation. The saddle of one surface became the valley of the other. The intersection of singly-folded structures resulted in the formation of the folded frame. Structurally, the concentration of forces at the frame corners necessitated strengthening at these points. The students also discovered that the more folds there were in a frame, the closer it approximated an arch or a barrel vault (Figure 3), as in the case of multiply-folded flat surfaces. When folds were arranged in a pattern where the corner points of folded edges lay within a cylinder surface, the bending stresses could be sustained favourably. This occurred because the triangular surfaces of the folded barrel were inclined perpendicularly to the cylindrical surface -- in contrast to folded structures lying tangentially to the surface curvature.

In all classes of molluscs, ribbing appears in both radial and concentric lines on the shell surface. The direction of the ribbing is critical to the strength of the surface and it is this directionality that relates to the orientation of load and support to any structural form. Le Ricolais recognised this property when he designed two directional corrugations for a floor slab and proved that there is a relationship between strength, plate thickness and the directionality of corrugations. He also discovered that the more directions the structure spanned (2 way vs. 1 way ribbing), the less the structure deformed. Deformation could also be reduced if the surface structure occupied a larger volume of space, in order to increase its rise to span ratio; this structural strategy is the morphological characteristic of the giant clam shell, which occurs at the outer rims of the bivalve. Whereas the folding of the shell surface had the structural effect of increasing effective structural depth, the two-directional ribbing of the calcium carbonate in the seashells had the effect of reducing buckling lengths with increased interconnections per unit of surface area.

Figure 4

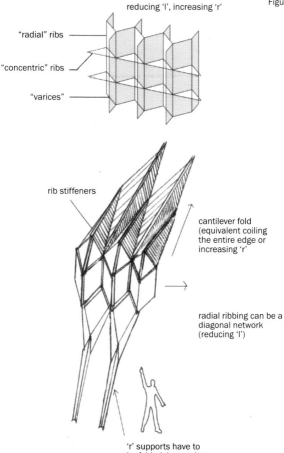

reducing 'l', increasing 'r'

"radial" ribs

"concentric" ribs

"varices"

rib stiffeners

cantilever fold
(equivalent coiling
the entire edge or
increasing 'r'

radial ribbing can be a
diagonal network
(reducing 'l')

'r' supports have to
be folded, increasing
'r' if 'l' is increased for
headroom or openings
for natural lighting

Figure 5

Shortening the buckling lengths improved the slenderness ratio which reduced the tendency of the surface structure to buckle under compression since slenderness ratio = $\frac{l}{r}$ (where 'r' was the radius of gyration). This formula suggested two possible ways of resisting buckling, or reducing the slenderness ratio of a compression member as illustrated in Figures 4, 5. Either 'r' was increased by thickening the member (as in the case of coiling its overall form or edge folding) or 'l' was decreased by reducing buckling length. It was this manipulation of 'l' and 'r' that gave each species its characteristic form and pattern, and that provided structural lessons for the studio prototypes.

Notes

1. Kenneth R. Wye, Illustrated Encyclopedia of Shells (London, Quarto Publishing, 1991).

2. In engineering terms, a shell is defined as a surface structure whose neutral plane (ie, the surface that halves the thickness of the shell at all points) is singly or doubly curved. Where the principal normal section is a straight line, the shell is singly curved. Similarly, where the principle normal section is a curve, the shell is doubly curved. A transverse shell is transverse to the longitudinal direction of the area to be covered. Its significance is in its small width (between edge beams) in relation to its span (between end panels). The resultant bending moments are small in comparison to those of a slab whose span is equal to the width of the shell. In longitudinal shells, the width between the edge beams is greater than the distance between the stiffening panels. Bending forces and edge disturbances are confined onto a small strip, with the greater part of the shell being stressed. The vaults of longitudinal shells require a width and height greater than transverse shells, for the same span-rise ratio.

3. According to Angerer, single-folded structures may intersect with each other to form a folded frame.

CRITICAL OBSERVATIONS ON PEDAGOGY

These studio projects were excellent vehicles in bridging structural theory with form making, whilst avoiding the appropriation of formal precedents based solely on appearance. Instead, students applied mathematical concepts such as that of slenderness ratio to the design and manipulation of the surface forms. The understanding of structural formulae as a guide to form making is a useful design tool for the designer.

The studios were not without certain difficulties, in particular, those associated with translation and modelling. The use of timber and cardboard as analogous modelling materials for shell structures was problematic since these surface structures are two-dimensional elastic forms. The ideal material for this kind of structure would allow for the formation of free forms or arbitrarily shaped surfaces, yet it would also be homogenous (ie. have an identical physical behaviour at all points). It would also be isotropic (ie. have an identical physical behaviour in all directions). Angerer observed that most known building materials are at best quasi-tropic. Natural materials such as timber have a definite grain, making them unsuitable for surface action, but plywood, when glued in thin layers with grain running in different directions, produced the effect of isotropy. Much effort was required for students to ensure surface (and structural) continuity in all the models throughout the design process.

Other issues emerged; for example, problems of form and shape arose where incongruent surfaces became mutually dependent. There was also the difficulty in modelling a true surface structure instead of one that acted as a structural frame. For example, the wires in the *nautilus* shell prototype needed to be secured at junctions of overlap in order for the entire arrangement to